THE FAMILY
HANDYMAN
DO-IT-YOURSELF
ENCYCLOPEDIA

THE FAMILY
HANDYMAN
DO-IT-
YOURSELF
ENCYCLOPEDIA

*Comprehensive How-To-Series
for the entire family...
containing material from
The Illustrated
Do-It-Yourself Encyclopedia
...written in simple language with
full step-by-step instructions
and profusely illustrated*

Illustrated Edition

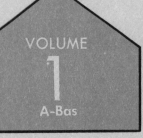

VOLUME

1

A-Bas

Published by arrangement with
Universal Publishing & Distributing
Corporation, Publisher of The
Family Handyman magazine.

How to Get the Most Out of This Encyclopedia

This encyclopedia is designed to meet the needs of the American family in today's do-it-yourself world.

Within these sixteen volumes, there are over 1,000 individual articles and more than 6,000 illustrations. The information contained herein will save you hours of time and labor and hundreds of dollars when you undertake do-it-yourself projects.

You need no special background to understand anything presented in these volumes. All technical and semi-technical terms are clearly defined in easy-to-understand language. All how-to projects are presented with step-by-step instructions and are profusely illustrated.

This comprehensive encyclopedia, covers all phases of do-it-yourself related to home improvement, maintenance and repair. In addition, there are many special topics of interest to the entire family. For father there are special sections on car care, darkroom layouts, Hi-Fi, to name but a few. For mother, your editors have included decorating ideas, kitchen space-savers, sewing centers, laundry rooms. And for the youngsters in the family, there are articles on bicycle care, bird houses, outdoor play centers and numerous projects to enable them to be full-fledged members of this do-it-yourself movement.

This encyclopedia is more than a how-to book; it is an idea book as well. In addition to telling the handyman and handywoman how to plan and how to do the specific job, there are idea sections included throughout.

Individualism is part of the American way of life. Everyone wants his home, inside and out, to be different from his neighbors'. Therefore, while including basic how-to instructions in step-by-step form, you will find many unusual photographs and sketches showing finished projects. There is an unlimited number of ways the attic in two identical homes can be finished. Here, in this encyclopedia, you have a reservoir of ideas not only for finishing attics but for many other topics as well.

Hundreds of authors have contributed to making this a basic how-to reference series for you. They are skilled craftsmen thoroughly versed in their respective fields. Many are the foremost authorities in the do-it-yourself movement. They are technical men, researchers, writers, home-owners, craftsmen and hobbyists.

Your editors have culled the many sources to collect all available information and to present it to every member of your family in an easy-to-understand form. They have used the services of professional educators versed in the presentation of instructional information. Furthermore, to aid in your complete understanding of any subject, your editors have included within these volumes numerous photographs and illustrations, many of which were prepared expressly for this encyclopedia.

Cognizant of the fact that there are many, many jobs for the do-it-yourself family to do and knowing that in some communities local laws and regulations prohibit anyone but a licensed professional from doing certain jobs, your editors have, in some instances, suggested that the handyman should *not* do the job himself. They recognize that some of the more advanced handymen can do these tasks easily. However, the legal and safety aspects have prompted your editors to include a warning note.

The alphabetical arrangement makes it easy to find the answers to an almost infinite number of perplexing how-to problems. There are also cross references to help you obtain additional information. Finally, the complete index in volume sixteen will help you locate quickly any information you need.

No longer need you be bewildered by some technical terms or search for an easy-to-understand solution to any how-to problem. Just pick up the volume, then do-it-yourself!

HAROLD JOSEPH HIGHLAND
Editorial Director

Prepared and Edited by

HOW-TO ASSOCIATES

With the Cooperation of the Editors of
Family Handyman Magazine

HAROLD J. HIGHLAND, B.S., M.S., PH.D., *Editorial Director*
E. R. HARRIS, B.A., *Executive Editor*
DOROTHY SARA, *Household Editor*
FRANK ROGERS, B.S., *Projects Editor*
PAUL M. CHEDA, *Art Director*
E. C. MOORE, *Staff Photographer*

How-To Associates is an organization composed of writers, technical and building consultants, photographers, artists and copywriters actively engaged in the do-it-yourself field. Not only have they written numerous how-to features which have appeared in newspapers the country over and in outstanding do-it-yourself magazines, but they have also worked with leading manufacturers of do-it-yourself materials and products.

Harold Joseph Highland, Editorial Director of How-To Associates, was formerly Editor of *The Family Handyman,* a Do-It-Yourself magazine for homeowners. He has written how-to features for many newspapers and popular magazines, including *Parade, Cars, Young Mechanic, The Family Mechanic* and for technical publications. He is the author and editor of "How to Double the Living Space of Your Home."

Dorothy Sara is a lecturer and author on subjects relating to home care, decorating and gardening. She is a member of the Women's National Book Association and among the books she has written are: "101 Ways to Increase the Value of Your Home," "New American Home Fix-It Book," "Bride's Encyclopedia," "Everybody's Home Fix-It Guide," "New American Garden Book."

Frank Rogers is an author of numerous how-to project features. He has written for *Living for Young Homemakers, The Family Handyman* and other publications.

CONSULTING EDITORIAL STAFF FOR THE
FAMILY HANDYMAN DO-IT-YOURSELF ENCYCLOPEDIA

How-To Editor . . . . . . RALPH TREVES

Well-known do-it yourself authority whose columns appear regularly in such leading newspapers as the *New York Daily Mirror, The Philadelphia Enquirer, The New York Times* and others throughout the United States. He contributes regularly to many do-it-yourself magazines and is the author of "Complete Book of Basement Improvements."

Architectural Editor . . . ROBERT B. STONE
S.B., Massachusetts Institute of Technology

Authority in home planning and building, he is president of Associated Plan Service of Huntington, N.Y. He is co-author of "The Complete Book of Home Modernizing" and author and editorial director of numerous volumes on home building and house planning, among which are "Low Cost Custom Homes," "New American Home Plans," "America Builds—Homes by Leading American Architects."

Engineering Editor . . . WILLIAM ATLAS
B.S., in Eng., C.E., School of Engineering, The City
College, Registered Professional Engineer

Expert in modern methods of construction, he is chief engineer with the Paul Weidlinger Co. Versed in new materials for home construction and modernizing as well as time- and money-saving techniques of building, he has worked on the development of many contemporary building projects. Writer of technical and do-it-yourself articles.

Heating and Plumbing Editor . . . ROBERT F. HEMBERGER
B.A., Long Island University, M.A., Columbia University

A technical expert in his field, he has written for scientific publications and he is also a do-it-yourself specialist writing for how-to magazines.

Industrial Consultant . . . LEON THEIL
B.S., *Columbia University*

Expert in industrial relations and marketing, he is well versed in do-it-yourself activities of the homeowner. In addition to his writing for the *Baltimore Sun* Magazine, he is a regular contributor of how-to features to *The Family Handyman*.

Educational Consultant . . . JEROME MARCUS
B.S., New Jersey State Teachers College,
M.A., New York University

Instructor of Industrial Arts at Cleveland Junior High School in Newark, New Jersey, he has acted as advisor in the preparation and presentation of specialized instructional information in the crafts field in this series.

Layout and Art . . . CHEDA STUDIOS AND
DiFRANZA WILLIAMSON ASSOCIATES

ACKNOWLEDGMENTS

The editors of this series would like to express their thanks and appreciation to the following companies for their assistance in preparing special sections within this volume, for their technical advice and their permission to use special material, photographs, art and educational charts.

ARMSTRONG CORK CO. • BAKELITE CO., DIVISION OF UNION CARBIDE AND CARBON CORP. • BEHR-MANNING CORP. • BICYCLE INSTITUTE OF AMERICA • BURGESS VIBROCRAFTERS, INC. • CALIFORNIA REDWOOD ASS'N. • CARRIER CORP. • CLAY POT MANUFACTURERS ASS'N. • CONSTAD LABORATORIES • CUMMINS OF JOHN OSTER MANUFACTURING CO. • DARRA-JAMES CO. • DEWALT, INC. • DOW CHEMICAL CO. • EPOXY COATING CO. • THE FORMICA COMPANY • THE MAJESTIC CO., INC. • MARSH WALL PRODUCTS, INC. • MASONITE CORP. • MIRACLE ADHESIVES • MODERNFOLD DOORS, NEW CASTLE PRODUCTS • NATIONAL COTTON COUNCIL • OWENS-CORNING FIBERGLASS CORP. • P & G SUPPLY CO. • PITTSBURGH PLATE GLASS CO. • RESIN SYSTEMS • REYNOLDS METALS COMPANY • RUBBER FLOORING DIVISION OF THE RUBBER MANUFACTURING ASSN. • SHELLAC INFORMATION BUREAU • SKIL CORP. • STANLEY TOOLS, DIVISION OF THE STANLEY WORKS • TENNESSEE EASTMAN CO. • TILE COUNCIL OF AMERICA • TURNER BRASS WORKS • UNITED STATES PLYWOOD CORP. • WEN PRODUCTS, INC. • WESTERN WOOD PRODUCTS ASS'N. • WOOD CONVERSION CO. • WOODHILL CHEMICAL CO.

For their combined efforts in revising this work, the Publishers wish to thank Morton Waters, Editorial Director of THE FAMILY HANDYMAN Magazine, and Patrick O'Rourke, of Morpad, Inc., Graphic Designers.

Abbreviations— Building Terms

The home handyman finds it helpful to know the abbreviations which are commonly used in the building trades. This information is of value when ordering lumber and other materials, reading house plans or project plans and estimates. Here are some of the more widely used abbreviations:

A.C.	alternating current
A.D.	air-dried
av.	average
av. l.	average length
av. w.	average width
bbl.	barrel
bd.	board
bd. ft.	board foot (1 sq. ft. by 1 in. thick)
bdl.	bundle
bev.	beveled
bgs.	bags
B.T.U.	British thermal unit
CL	center line
clg.	ceiling
clr.	clear
C.M.	c e n t e r m a t c h e d (tongue - and - groove joints are made along center of the edge)
com.	common
csg.	casing
ctg.	crating
cu. ft.	cubic foot
cu. in.	cubic inch (or cubic inches)
cu. yd.	cubic yard (or cubic yards)
d.	nail size (penny)
D.C.	direct current
D & CM	dressed (1 or 2 sides) and center matched
D & M	dressed and matched (dressed 1 or 2 sides, and tongued - and - grooved on edges. The match may be center or standard.)
D & SM	dressed (1 or 2 sides) and standard matched
D 2S & M	dressed 2 sides and (center or standard) matched
D 2S & SM	dressed 2 sides and standard matched
deg. (or °)	degrees
dia.	diameter
dim.	dimension
D.S.	drop siding
E.	edge
Fahr. (or F.)	Fahrenheit
FAS	firsts and seconds (combined grade of the 2 upper grades of hardwoods)
f. bk.	flat back
facty.	factory (lumber)
F.G.	flat grain
flg.	flooring
f.o.k.	free of knots
frm.	framing
ft. (or ′)	foot (or feet)
gal.	gallon (or gallons)
hdl.	handle (stock)
hdwd.	hardwood
H.P.	horsepower
hrt.	heart
hrtwd.	heartwood
in. (or ″)	inch (or inches)
KD	kiln-dried
k.d.	knocked down
lbr.	lumber
lgth.	length
lin. ft.	linear foot (12 inches)
L.R.	long run

Lr. MCO	long run, mill culls out
manuf.	manufacturer
M.	one thousand
M.b.m.	1000 ft. board measure
M.R.	mill run
M.s.m.	1000 ft. surface measure
m.w.	mixed width
No. or #	number
nt. wt.	net weight
1s & 2s	ones and twos (combined grade of the hardwood grades of firsts and seconds)
ord.	order
oz.	ounce (or ounces)
P.	planed
pat.	pattern
pln.	plain (as in plain sawed)
pn.	partition
qtd.	quartered (referring to hardwoods)
rd.	round
rdm.	random
res.	resawed
rfg.	roofing
rfrs.	roofers
rip.	ripped
r.l.	random length
R.P.M.	revolutions per minute
r.w.	random width
S & E	surfaced 1 side and 1 edge
S 1E	surfaced 1 edge
S1S1E	surfaced 1 side and 1 edge
S1S2E	surfaced 1 side and 2 edges
S 2 E	surfaced 2 edges
S 4 S	surfaced 4 sides
S & CM	surfaced 1 or 2 sides and center matched
S & M	surfaced and matched (surfaced 1 or 2 sides, and tongued - and - grooved on edges. The match may be center or standard.)
S & SM	surfaced 1 or 2 sides and standard matched
S2S & CM	surfaced 2 sides and center matched
S2S & M	surfaced 2 sides and standard or center matched
S2S & SM	surfaced 2 sides and standard matched
sp.	sapwood
SB	standard bead
sd.	seasoned
sdg.	siding
sel.	select
S.E.Sd.	square-edge siding
s.f.	surface feet (an area of 1 sq ft.)
sftwd.	softwood
sh.d.	shipping dry
ship.	shiplap
Sm.	standard matched
s.m.	surface measure
s.n.d.	sap no defect
snd.	sound
sq.	square
sq. E.	square edge
Sq. E & S	square edge and sound
sqrs.	squares
S.S.	single strength
std.	standard
stk.	stock
S.W.	sound wormy
T & G	tongued-and-grooved
TB & S	top, bottom, and sides
tbrs.	timbers
V.G.	vertical grain
w.a.l.	wider, all length
wdr.	wider
wt.	weight
wth.	width
x	multiplied by
yd.	yard (or yards)

Abrasives

Also see *OILSTONES* and *SHARPENING TECHNIQUES*.

There are many different types of abrasives available to the home handyman today. Most people are familiar with "sandpaper," but steel-wool and mineral blocks also fall within this class. The term "sandpaper," meaning paper coated with abrasive grains, had its birth many years ago, probably when sand was actually used in that way. Today five different mineral grains are used, of various degrees of hardness and toughness, and the term "sandpaper" actually no longer describes the product.

Belt sanders are available in two forms—portable and stationary. A belt sander is particularly useful to speed the work. You can use a belt sander with any type of abrasive paper and for a variety of work.

Photo courtesy of Behr-Manning Corp.

Types of Sandpaper

Coated abrasives are almost the least expensive of the tools in your kit. The slight investment in maintaining a stock of the sizes and types you need, pays off in time saved, greater convenience and better work.

FOR REMOVING OLD PAINT —Flint paper is recommended for the job. There is little advantage in using a harder, sharper abrasive since the rapid loading of paint chips dictates the life of the paper. Use coarse grit for first rough sanding and medium grit for the second. Flint paper can be used for final sanding but other papers do a better job.

FOR WOOD—Garnet paper is the preferred choice for hand sanding and finishing wood. It comes in an assortment of grits. The following are the popular grit choices for the various stages of sanding: Very Coarse—1/2; Coarse—0; Medium —2/0; Fine—4/0 and Very Fine— 6/0.

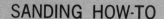

SANDING HOW-TO

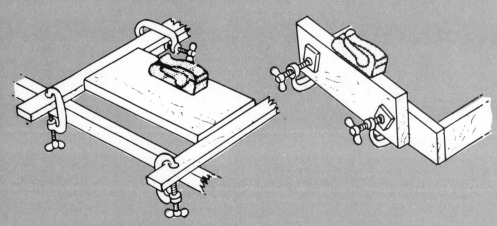

1. To sand a large flat surface, use two strips of wood secured in place with "C" clamps.

2. To sand an edge, set board in a vise or clamp it to the side of an upturned box.

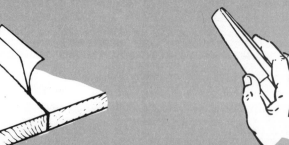

5. To reduce spots when butting two boards for gluing, slip folded piece of paper between them.

6. To sand a curved surface, use a tapered sanding stick, store-bought or shop-made.

Sketches courtesy of Behr-Manning Corp.

FOR RUST REMOVAL—Emery cloth is usually satisfactory where the job is not too extensive or only a small amount of rust has to be removed. Emery cloth ranks with flint paper as an abrasive for use in those cases where enduring sharpness is not required. If there is an excessive amount of rust, it is best to use a wire brush or wire wheel with an electric drill.

FOR POLISHING METAL SURFACES—Crocus cloth will give you a mirror finish on metal parts. It is widely used on gun actions, fishing reels and the like where frictionless smooth movement is essential.

FOR METAL PREPARATION AND FINISHING—Cloth with an aluminum oxide base such as Metalite, is best when preparing metal for a paint or lacquer finish. It is available in sheets, discs, rolls and other convenient forms for use.

FOR HARDWOODS AND METALS—Paper and cloth such as Ada-

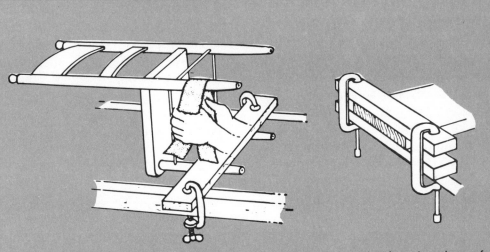

3. To sand chair legs, set chair on a side and "lock" it in place with a board and clamps.

4. To sand end grain, clamp two pieces of wood to top and bottom of board and to work bench.

7. Wet sanding is best for primers and between coats when finishing with varnish or enamel.

8. To crease sandpaper, pull with grain up over a sharp corner once or twice as shown.

lox offer the handyman a sharp, hard and enduring abrasive for finishing. It is particularly good with power sanders and can also be used for hand sanding operations. Because of its long cutting life, the sanding is seldom interrupted for renewing this type of abrasive.

FOR PLASTICS, COMPOSITION MATERIALS AND METALS—Durite paper, coated with diamond-hard silicon carbide grit, is exceptionally sharp. In its waterproof form, it is most valuable for wet sanding primers and undercoats for enamel, lacquer and other surfacing materials.

FOR FLOOR FINISHING — Special grit paper is available for floor sanding machines, which are often available on a rental basis from the local hardware store. For old floors, start by sanding with Very Coarse or Coarse paper, 3½ or 4 grit. Follow this with a Fine paper, ½ and give the floors a final sanding with Very Fine floor sanding paper, 2/0. On the other hand, with new floors, either softwood or hardwood, start with Medium grit paper, 2½ and then use Fine, ½, finishing with Very Fine floor paper.

Sanding Techniques

The first step in reducing sanding effort is to select the right coated abrasive for the job. That is, the one which will cut sharpest and fastest.

The second step is to hold the work steady. This may seem like an obvious requirement, but it is too often neglected. Note the accompanying sketches for a few suggestions for doing this job. Do not hold the work in one hand and sand with the other; it is best to avoid muscular fatigue before you start.

Always use a backing surface for the abrasive paper when sanding. Use a sanding block, even a convenient piece of wood, or a power sander; never just your hand.

When using a power sander, cut the abrasive paper or cloth to the proper size so that it covers the entire sanding pad.

GUIDE TO ABRASIVE BELT SELECTION

TYPE OF WOOD	ROUGH	FINISH	FINE FINISH
Birch	2½—1	½—0	2/0—4/0
Cypress	2½—1½	½—0	2/0
Fir	1½—1	½—0	2/0
Gum	2½—1½	½—0	2/0—3/0
Mahogany	2½—1½	½—0	2/0—3/0
Maple	2½—1	½—0	2/0—4/0
Maple (curly)	2½—1½	½—0	2/0—4/0
Oak	2½—1½	½—0	2/0—4/0
Walnut	2½—1½	½—0	2/0—4/0
White pine	1½—1	0	2/0
Yellow pine	2 —1½	½	0

Courtesy of Porter Cable, Inc.

An inexpensive hand sander helps you get the most out of the abrasive paper you're using. It is scientifically designed to relieve the fingers from that tiring job of holding the paper and it fits comfortably in the palm.

Circular sanding discs are handy with an electric drill. The abrasive disc is backed by a rubber pad, giving it flexibility and yet firmness. Keep sander in motion on any surface, especially when using a coarse paper.

There are many types of "flat" sanders the handyman can use; these include the orbital for uniform sanding, straight line for finishing and the reciprocating type, especially useful for smoothing edges of wood pieces.

Photo courtesy of Wen Products

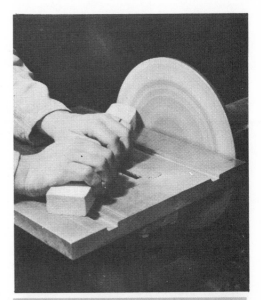

There are special disc sanders available, but the home handyman can convert his saw into a stationary disc sander. Merely take out the blade and replace it with a disc to which a piece of abrasive paper is glued for use.

Photo courtesy of Behr-Manning Corp.

ABRASIVES AND THEIR USES

TYPE	USE	COLOR	HARDNESS*
Aluminum oxide	hardwood and metals	reddish-brown	9
Crocus	polishing metal to a mirror finish	dull red to purple	2
Emery	on any small, quick sanding job	dull black	8
Flint	. . . . see quartz		
Garnet	softwood and hardwood	red	7
Pumice	final polishing and to cut down (roughen slightly) finishing coats of varnish, etc.	off-white	4
Quartz	to remove old paint and furniture finish	grayish-white	6
Rottenstone	furniture polishing and roughing down varnish and shellac coats	off-white	3
Rouge	polishing of metal	red or green	0
Silicon carbide	fine finishing of wood; also on plastics and metal	gray, green or black	1-10

* The grading of hardness is an indication of the hardness of the abrasive itself and not the grading value of the abrasive paper made of these grains.

SELECTING THE RIGHT ABRASIVE FOR THE JOB

MATERIAL	ABRASIVE	SANDING		
		ROUGH	MEDIUM	FINE
Aluminum	Aluminum oxide	40	80	100
Brass	Silicon carbide	40	80	120
Composition board	Garnet	1	½	0
Copper	Aluminum oxide	40	80	120
Cork	Garnet	3	1	0
Glass	Silicon carbide	50	120	320
Hardwood	Aluminum oxide or garnet	2½	½	3/0
Iron	Silicon carbide	30	60	100
Paint (removal)	Flint	2	½	. . .
Softwood	Garnet	1½	0	2/0
Steel	Aluminum oxide	30	60	100

Note: Grit is the designation of the number of grains which, when set end to end, equals one inch, as 120, 320. Numbers like ½ and 1 are arbitrary designations.

Accident Prevention

Put your garden tools away as soon as you're finished. If these must be around, keep the sharp, cutting edges facing the ground.

Safety first is the rule for all members of the family, in and around the house. Safety is no accident! It is the practice of common sense, following certain basic rules and eliminating or minimizing hazards. It is especially essential for the do-it-yourself handyman to follow safety rules. No job should be undertaken without full knowledge of what must be done, the right tools needed for the job and awareness of possible hazards.

It is essential to understand what causes accidents if you are to be successful in preventing them. Never do any do-it-yourself project unless you are fully awake and alert. Fatigue increases your reaction time, and in that split second, you may have an accident.

Color Safety Code

A sane system of warning through color which is used on highways and in factories, may be adapted for use in and around the home. Use these colors, which are universally accepted in safety codes, and have each member of the family learn what each one stands for.

• Yellow, or yellow and black alternate stripes, are used where there is any low protruding beam, or for stairway approaches, or any sudden ledges on the floor. Therefore, yellow (or yellow and black stripes) is the warning sign for "don't bump your head, or don't stumble or fall."

• Orange is the color to paint to attract attention. It is a warning sign for extra caution. Paint it on the inside of your fuse box or in any spot where there is electrical equipment or moving machinery.

• Green is the universal safety color, and is painted on the first aid kit or any

Safety green—this universal safety color should be used to identify first aid kits or cabinets with supplies needed for emergencies.

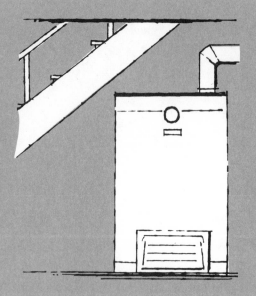

High-visibility yellow—use yellow and black stripes to mark tripping, stumbling or strike-against hazards in the home.

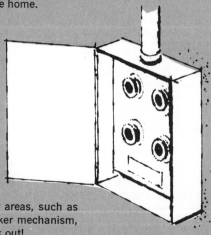

Alert orange—paint danger areas, such as inside of fuse boxes or stoker mechanism, with this warning color: look out!

other container or cabinet containing material for aiding in the time of accident or illness.

● Red is the usual danger signal, and it should be used for designing fire-fighting equipment and any other devices you may have for combatting a fire hazard.

● Blue is designated as the color to mark any electrical or other equipment which is in need of repair. You can hang a blue cardboard or other marker, so that the family will be warned not to use that damaged equipment until it has been repaired and the blue warning sign removed.

● White or gray gives a choice for the housekeeper or the home handyman in the workshop to designate waste receptacle areas. Thus, it promotes tidiness when working in the house and no waste is left around. It is always the white or gray area where a suitable receptacle with a cover is found.

Fire protection red—this danger signal color should be used to designate any fire-fighting equipment you have in your home.

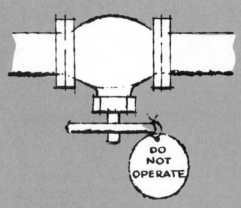

Precaution blue—this is a warning color used to identify an item in need of repair; it's a warning: don't touch!

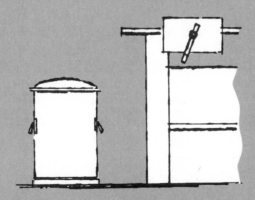

Clean white—this is a call to cleanliness, used to specify waste receptacle areas, especially useful in the workshop.

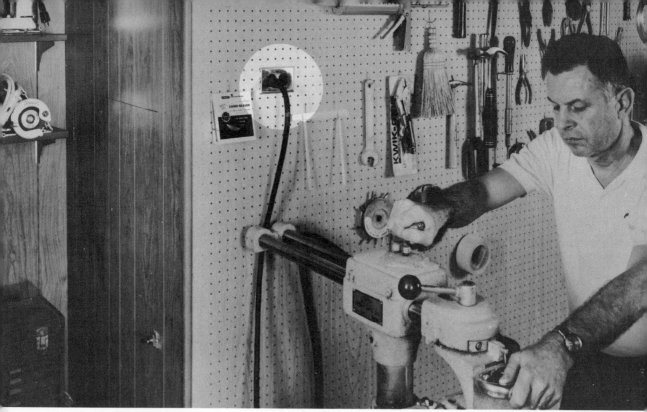

Photo courtesy of Masonite Peg-Board

Electrical Hazards

Wherever electrical appliances, lighting fixtures, wiring and outlets are located, indoors or outdoors, caution must be exercised in testing, repairing or replacing them.

Faulty house wiring, broken or frayed cords, damaged sockets and switches are dangerous. If you have any doubts about their efficiency and safety, replace them at once!

Never undertake any electrical repair in the house without first shutting off the electrical current. If you know which fuse controls the line on which you plan to work, remove that fuse. Take it out of the fuse box; just don't unscrew it part of the way. It is best to put the fuse away, somewhere removed from the fuse box and to hang a note on the fuse box to warn anyone that electrical work is being done and not to put a fuse in on the line. If you don't know which fuse controls the line, pull the master

> Even a well-planned workshop such as this one, is not a safe place to work unless properly laid out for easy access. Good lighting is another necessity. Be sure all outlets used to power your tools are adequately grounded and protected by fuses or circuit breakers.

switch and shut off all the current.

Fires often occur through overheating of wires which are carrying too much current or because of an electric arc in the presence of combustible material. Therefore do not use too many appliances on any one line or plug them into one outlet by using a multiple extension cord.

Remember: the blowing of a fuse is a sign—a warning that your circuit is carrying too much current. It may only be a temporary overload, but even a momentary overload is sufficient to blow a fuse. If your fuse blows, play it safe—examine the load the line is carrying.

Do not purchase appliances

marked "A.C. only" if the current in your house is D.C.; in that case, you can buy either D.C. or A.C. and D.C. appliances. A motor (by itself or in an appliance) that works on both A.C. and D.C. is called a universal motor. Look at the label of approval of the Board of Underwriters' Laboratories, before buying, to be sure that it is a safe appliance for your home.

If your hands are wet, don't touch any appliance. The same goes if you're standing on a wet spot. This is especially true in the bathroom, kitchen or laundry room. All handles on an appliance should be covered with insulating material (generally plastic) and not left as an exposed metal part.

Do not answer the telephone unless your hands are dry. It may look glamourous to see a movie where the telephone is in the bathroom, but in actual practice, this constitutes an electrical hazard.

Don't use long cords all around the room. Add extra outlets if you need them. Cords stretched around the room are potential fire hazards, particularly dangerous if run under a carpet or rug. The long wires are also dangerous for toddlers.

If you use a portable extension cord with a light attached to it, whether it be in the garage or basement or in the workshop, keep the light away from anything combustible, like paper or a thin curtain. A wire "cage" should always be used around the bulb, for accident prevention.

Also see *ELECTRICAL WIRING SAFETY RULES*.

Protect yourself from shock when using tools—a screwdriver or pliers—by coating the handles with an insulating plastic cover.

Photo courtesy Resin Systems, Inc.

If you use a portable light, keep it away from anything combustible. Use a wire "cage" around the bulb for added protection.

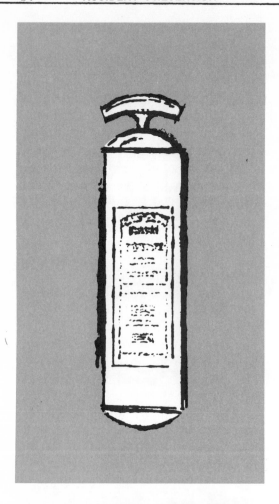

Fire Hazards

Rubbish, waste paper and other combustible materials should not be collected near the house. They should be kept in safe covered metal receptacles and burned before any large amount accumulates.

Bonfires, too, are hazards and should not be left to "burn out by themselves" but must be watched until the very end. It is best not to burn rubbish or have a bonfire any closer to the house than fifty feet. Dried grass, too, must not be left to accumulate. As it dries, it generates heat and can ignite. If you cannot dispose of dried grass in any other way, burn it.

Some plastics, celluloid and all other similar materials as well as photographic films are highly combustible. Be cautious about smoking, lighting matches or having these materials near an open fire or fireplace.

Basements and attics are rubbish-accumulating centers and are to be considered danger spots where fire is concerned. Give these extra rooms or storage spots periodic check-ups and clear out all non-essential materials.

Chimneys, flues, fireplaces and smokepipes must be cleaned regularly in order to remove the accumulated soot. Defective chimneys and flues are causes of unnecessary fires in the home. Any defects or damages should be repaired instantly.

A close-meshed wire or fire screen should always be kept in front of the fireplace. It is best to avoid combustible flooring next to the fireplace; instead, have the floor near the fireplace made of tiles, stone or brick. Also avoid throwing excelsior or large quantities of paper or other flammable materials into the fireplace to burn; it's too exposed for safety in the home.

Portable hand fire-extinguishers are available for use in and around the home. When buying such items, be certain that they bear the seal of approval of the Board of Underwriters' Laboratories.

If you have no extinguisher available and a fire breaks out, call the Fire Department or Police Department at once. Get everyone out of the house. It is more important to save a life than to try to rescue some material possessions.

The prompt application of water or the use of blankets thrown over the blaze may be effective in extinguishing a small fire before it has a chance to grow into something disasterous. Use a pail, partially filled with water. Or even a broom soaked in water may often be used with good results to beat out a small blaze. A garden hose is, of course, an excellent fire-fighter to have on hand. There are fog nozzles, easily attached to the hose, to combat home fire.

Also see *FIRE PROTECTION*.

Rags which contain grease, oil or paint must not be kept around. If left unprotected, they present a fire hazard. Always clean up after you have painted and dispose of all paint-soaked rags. If you must store them, keep them in a tightly closed container. A mason jar is exceedingly handy for such purposes. It has a tightly-sealed screwcap cover. Because it's made of glass, you can easily see what's stored inside. But because it's made of glass, it's easily breakable. Keep such jars away from shelf edges and other locations where there is danger of breakage. If you use metal containers with tight covers for such storage, label the contents on the outside of the can.

Ladder Safety

Although no actual statistics are available, accidents involving ladders rate high. A good ladder is one of the most useful accessories for the handyman, but it must be used properly. Safety is important whether you are a housewife using a small stepladder in the kitchen or you are a home handyman using a 30′ extension ladder outside the house to paint the trim.

Whether using a ladder indoors or outdoors, you can avoid accidents by observing a few simple rules.

1. While aluminum or magnesium ladders are easier to handle than wood ones, remember that metal is a conductor of electricity. It is important to keep a metal ladder from coming into contact with electric power lines.

2. Don't paint the ladder; the color will keep you from noticing such defects as cracks or splits.

3. The safest angle for a ladder is to place the feet of the ladder about a quarter of its length away from the wall. For example, a 15-foot ladder should be set away (on its feet) about 4 feet from the wall.

4. Make certain that the ladder is on firm ground and won't slip. If you use a metal ladder and rest it on concrete walk or driveway, use rubber-bottom safety feet with the ladder. If you use a wood ladder, it should have rubber "feet" permanently attached to the bottom of it.

5. Make sure that the top of the ladder, against the wall, is also braced properly and not on a surface where it will slide. Don't put the top of a ladder so that it rests against a screen or window pane.

Play it safe on ladders! Never use a ladder outdoors on a windy day. If you are using a stepladder and need both hands free to work, do not go higher than the second step from the top on high stepladders or the next to the top on shorter ladders.

6. A ladder on a roof must be thoroughly secured, and for this purpose you can obtain roof hooks to attach to the ladder at any hardware store.

7. Don't set your ladder up so that it is directly in front of a door. If that position is necessary, lock the door and put a warning sign on it. It is a better idea to have someone stand by to make certain that the door is

not inadvertently opened.

8. Never climb an extension ladder or any long ladder on a very windy day. If you must use the ladder then, have someone hold the base of the ladder as you climb up, stay up there and work and when you climb down again afterwards.

9. An easy way to carry a ladder is to paint a strip at the center of it, then take hold of the ladder and you'll have an even balance.

10. When climbing a ladder, face the ladder, going up and coming down, and take one step at a time.

11. If you're working high up, don't go any higher than the third rung from the top of the ladder and always wear skid-proof soled shoes. If you're using a step ladder, do not stand on the top step; the highest you should go is the second step from the top on a tall stepladder, over 3 feet, or next to the top on shorter ladders.

12. A chore which needs both hands, such as hanging storm sash or screens, must be figured out beforehand, so that you don't teeter on the ladder with your hands holding heavy or swaying objects. Have someone pass them up to you, or perhaps you can pull them up with a rope.

13. If you need both hands for a quick job, grab hold of a rung of the ladder with your leg, or perhaps pass your elbow through a convenient rung.

14. Don't try to reach over too far, when on a ladder. It's best to get off and to move the ladder the few inches. Don't hold a paint can when you're on the ladder; provide a hook on which to hang the can.

15. If you own an extension ladder, and want to raise or lower it, brace the base of the ladder (on the ground) against your foot, and holding on to the ladder, lift it away from the house with one hand until it is almost vertical. Holding it with one hand, use the other hand to pull the rope which extends the ladder.

16. Furthermore, check the rope on your extension ladder periodically to see that there are no weak spots.

Power Saw, Safe Usage

This tool which enables you to do a craftsmanlike job is perfectly safe to use, provided you are careful. When you make measurements while a piece of wood is in the saw, be sure that the electric switch is off or that the motor is disconnected from the outlet.

Keep the height of the blade properly adjusted, because if it is too high it may be dangerous; two saw-teeth above the top surface of the wood being cut is a safe guide.

Make a periodical check to see that the blade is tight on the arbor. Disconnect the motor from the outlet when inspecting or working on the blade. Make certain that you don't jam the blade when tightening it; instead, hold the belt to prevent the arbor from rotating.

The control knob of the power saw must be kept in working order. Every two months lubricate the wheel controls with graphite.

When cutting (that is, ripping) along the grain of a wide piece of wood, protect yourself by straddling the rip fence with the fingers of your hand.

But in ripping narrow pieces of wood, keep your fingers away from the blade; instead, use a pusher stick to guide and push the wood through the saw blade and the rip fence.

Radio and Television Sets

Care must be taken to avoid contact with, or crossing over or under electric power, light, telephone, or telegraph conductors, when you erect an antenna. Fatal shock is often caused by contact between power conductors and antenna wires.

If your outdoor radio or TV antennas are not grounded, disconnect them during a lightning storm, and connect them to an effective ground. Information regarding safe grounding is contained in the National Electrical Safety Code. A lightning arrester could be connected to the lead-in wire from an outside antenna.

Always be sure that the set is disconnected from the supply circuit, before you replace pilot lights or tubes in a radio or TV.

When taking a television set apart to make needed repairs, follow safe and sane rules. Not only must you disconnect the plug from the wall outlet, but you should ground the high voltage element within the set. See *TELEVISION*.

Stairways

Whether outdoor or indoor stairways, they must be kept clear of toys, bundles, rubbish. Tripping on stairs is one of the most common household accidents.

Dark stairways leading to an attic or a basement should be adequately lighted with a switch placed at the bottom and at the top of the stairway to control the light. The bottom and top stairs should be painted, preferably yellow as mentioned in the **Color** section, or in some other light color. If you do not wish to paint the entire step, paint a narrow band, about 1" wide, along the outer edge.

A handrail or banister must be provided on all stairways, especially those leading to porches outdoors because of the danger in wet or icy weather.

Many accidents occur on stairways, but you'll be safe with adequate lighting and a top and bottom step painted in yellow or a light color where lighting is bad.

Accordion-Fold Doors

In the average six room house, ordinary swinging doors waste about 90 square feet of floor space and a great deal more of wall space. This is equivalent to an extra small bedroom. Contemporary accordion-fold doors, like "Modernfold," save the space wasted by swinging doors. The folding doors open and close inside the doorway and permit better use of wall and floor areas.

In addition to their space-saving qualities, these doors have many uses within the home. They can be used as room dividers, to separate living from sleeping quarters, to divide a bedroom in half—a game area and a sleeping area or two sleeping areas for a young boy and another for a young girl.

Modern folding doors are easily installed by the home handyman. Many different models are available on the market. The only tools you need for the job are a screwdriver and drill and bit. If the track is too long, however, you'll also need a hacksaw to cut the metal and a metal file to smooth off the rough edges.

Many of the folding doors available today are easy to blend into any room's decorating scheme. The doors are available in a wide assortment of colors in washable vinyl plastic. However, if you change your mind after you've installed one, you have two choices:

- first, you can use a quality rubber base paint and change the door's color to match or contrast with the room's trim or wall

- or, secondly, you can cover the folding door with fabric. This is done without any sewing. For how-to details you can apply to the manufacturer or dealer from whom you purchased the door.

What To Do with Old Door

No need to throw away your old swinging door when you install a folding door. If you're a handyman about the house and have but a few simple hand tools, you can put that old door to use. There are many handsome furniture pieces you can build yourself.

For suggested uses of old doors, see *FLUSH DOOR PROJECTS*.

1. Fit aluminum track to door opening and cut it to size with a hacksaw. Mark and drill holes in top of door jamb to match the track.

HOW TO INSTALL

CONTEMPORARY

ACCORDION-FOLD

DOORS

2. Remove door from carton and slide track into the nylon slides while the door is in the stack position.

3. Lift door and track so that track holes are aligned with those previously drilled in top of door frame. Screw track in place.

4. Move door away from fixed jamb or wall. With screws provided, secure jamb clips after lining them up with slots in door jamb post.

5. Press jamb post (closed edge of the folding door) over the jamb clips so that they are securely "locked" in place.

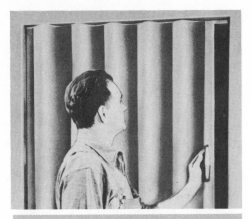

6. Lubricate the inside lips and bottom of lip of track with the lubricant supplied with the door. Move door back and forth.

8. Or you can match the door to your drapery or upholstery fabric. No sewing is necessary. Literature is available from your dealer.

7. You can paint the door to match any color in the room provided you apply a good rubber base paint according to directions on the can.

Add a corner closet in a room with inadequate storage facilities. Shoes and hats take up a lot of space, but you can give them a closet all their own. An accordion-fold door across one corner of the room makes a wonderful "no rummaging" hat and shoe storage area.

No need to waste the space under-the-eaves in the attic. Use that valuable space —folding doors will finish it off into a compact, easily accessible storage room.

Photos and sketches courtesy of Modernfold Doors, New Castle Products

If you wish to conceal that bar in your basement when it's not in use, here's an easy and convenient way to do the job. A locking folding door will keep the youngsters away.

Adhesives

There's a lot more to using an adhesive than merely applying it to the surface of the pieces to be joined. With the proper adhesive you can get a bonding that is stronger than the material itself.

Before proceeding, it should be noted that there are many different types of adhesives. Some are designed to do a specialized job while others can be used for several purposes. Some adhesives or glues bond instantly and require no clamping while others set more slowly and the work must be clamped until the adhesive is thoroughly dry.

There are adhesives for bonding any one material to any other material. They bond in two ways. Either the adhesive enters the pores of the material; this is technically known as mechanical adhesion. On the other hand, the adhesive may stay on the surface of a non-porous material; this is known as surface tension adhesion.

Adhesives and Their Uses

Casein glue—This is one of the few glues you can use in a cold workshop, even on rough wood and poorly fitted joints. It comes in powder form and is mixed with cold water, usually 1 part adhesive to 2 parts water (by weight). For best results, leave mixture stand for about 15 minutes and then stir again and apply. It's safe to use at any temperature above freezing and only moderate clamping pressure is necessary. Here's a time guide—hardwoods take at least 5

There are many different types of clamps which the home handyman can use to hold the work while the adhesive is drying. Here are a few of the more commonly used clamps which you can find in most handyman workshops: (clockwise, starting at the top) pipe clamp, hand screw, small bar clamp and a large C-clamp. Each has a specific purpose when used with adhesives in the workshop.

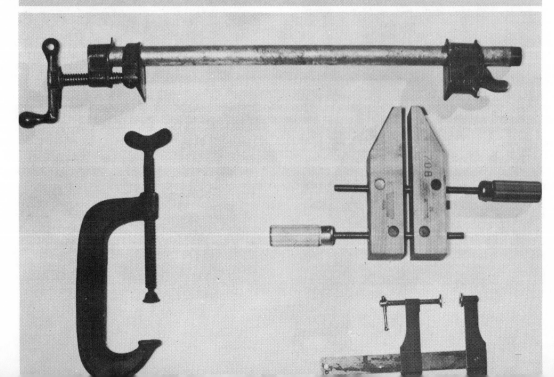

hours and softwoods about 3 hours for the adhesive to set when clamps are used.

Casein, flexible latex—Here's one to bond really difficult-to-glue materials. It can be used to join metal and other non-porous materials to wood and other porous and semiporous materials to each other.

Cellulose cement—This is a fast drying, transparent adhesive that is best suited for small repair work, such as china mending, or for model building. It comes already prepared, generally in a tube for instant application.

Epoxy—A product of modern science, this material is capable of producing bonds of fantastic strength. It can be used to fasten any two materials. Because it is quite costly, however, it is not often used in large amounts but is ideal for repairs where a small dab will do. Packaged in squeeze tubes by many manufacturers. Most epoxies have two components—a resin and a hardener—in separate tubes. They are not mixed until ready to proceed because they have a limited pot life. Setting time can range from an hour to a full day.

Hot hide glue—Although not generally used by home handymen today for gluing about the house, it is an old adhesive that still does an excellent job. You can buy hide glue in cake, flake or ground forms. Soak the glue in lukewarm water overnight—1 part glue to 2 parts water, by weight or according to the maker's instructions. Use glass ovenware or metal containers double-boiler fashion to keep it below 150° F, and apply hot. Heat only the quantity needed; frequent reheating weakens the glue. It sets fast, but requires

Always protect the face or surface of the wood from the metal edge of the clamp. As you apply pressure the metal will "eat" into the wood if you don't use a protective block.

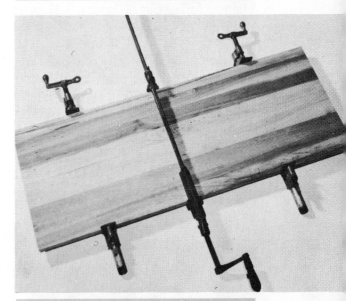

Alternate pipe or bar clamps when you glue boards edge of edge. Remember to sand the edges between boards perfectly smooth before applying the adhesive and adding the clamps.

tight clamping and matched joints for proper bonding.

Liquid fish glue—It is convenient to use as it comes already mixed in liquid form. If, however, it's too thick, you can "thin" it by setting the jar in a pan of hot water; but don't boil! After applying the adhesive to the pieces to be joined, wait for about 5 to 10 minutes before closing the joint. Clamp the work and let it stay undisturbed for at least 24 hours.

Liquid hide glue—Stronger than wood, this glue is fast setting and can be used anywhere so long as the temperature is higher than 60 degrees. In many ways it's similar to hot glue, but is more foolproof. It can be used for a wide variety of work.

Resorcinol resin—A room-temperature setting adhesive, works well indoors and out, in hot or cold. Joints with this type of adhesive are very durable. Leaving the work under clamps for about 8 hours will produce a long-lasting joint. This adhesive is sold as a thick liquid with a separate powered catalyst, which are mixed together just prior to using.

Synthetic rubber and resin—There are several different classes of adhesives in this group. There is the instant bonding group that joins two pieces when only moderate pressure is applied for only a few moments. Furthermore, there is the sensitive structural type, which requires a minimum of clamping. Finally, there is a general purpose thermoplastic type made of synthetic rubber and resin.

The instant type is used basically for bonding plastic laminated surfaces, such as Formica, Micarta, Consoweld. The general purpose combination is highly versatile; it can be used not only to join like materials, but also to join one type with another, including: metal, wood, plastic, fabric, ceramic, rubber, leather, plaster, glass, cement, etc.

Urea resin—Available in powder form, this type of adhesive is mixed with cold water, generally 10 parts glue to 6 parts water. Unlike casein glue, this adhesive can be used as soon as it's mixed. However, once mixed, it should not be kept for more than 6 to 7 hours. Workroom, wood

One technique of holding the legs of a chair in position while the adhesive is drying is to use a special glass filament tape. It's very handy to apply pressure on any surface.

Ordinary rope will do the trick as well when it's necessary to clamp chair legs while the glue is setting. Take up on the rope slack by twisting a small stick; tie securely.

glue and curing temperature should be 70° F or higher. Well fitted joints and high clamping pressure are required.

White polyvinyl liquid glue— Relatively new in the adhesives family, this type has become exceedingly popular because of its convenience, speed in setting, and stain-proof quality. Available in both squeeze tube and bottle, this adhesive dries transparent and sets within a half hour. Very little clamping pressure is needed. This is a fine many-purpose adhesive, but is not moistureproof or heat resistant although different brands may vary to some extent in this respect.

Vise clamps, generally used to hold pieces of wood for nailing, are exceptionally useful as gluing clamps. By using this type of clamp, you are assured of a perfectly square joint.

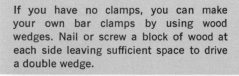

If you have no clamps, you can make your own bar clamps by using wood wedges. Nail or screw a block of wood at each side leaving sufficient space to drive a double wedge.

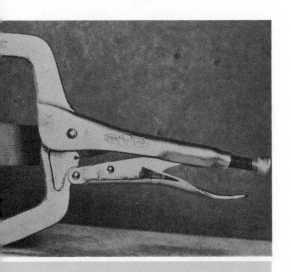

"C" clamp pliers are likewise very useful in place of the ordinary "C" clamp. A mere twist of the set screw on the edge of the handle make the clamp jaws larger or smaller.

This master chart shows six kinds of

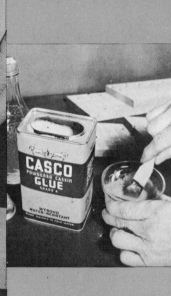

Type of Glue
Liquid Hide and Fish Glue
Brands include LePage's Liquid Glue, Franklin Liquid Glue and Rogers Isenglass.

Good for
Furniture and cabinetwork, general wood gluing.

Not Good for
Outdoor furniture and anything exposed to dampness.

Advantages
Strong, easy to use, light color, fills cracks and gaps in joints, resists heat, mold.

Disadvantages
It is not water resistant, must be warmed if used in a cold location or in cold weather.

Type of Glue
Powdered Casein
Brands include Casco LePage's Casein Glue.

Good for
General woodworking, especially oily woods: teak, yew, lemon.

Not Good for
Acid woods unless staining is not important; outdoor furniture.

Advantages
Strong, fairly water resistant, works in cool locations, fills cracks and poor joints.

Disadvantages
Must be mixed 15 minutes before using, subject to mold, stains dark woods.

Type of Glue
Resorcinol
Brands include Cascophen, U.S. Plywood Phenol Resorcinol Glue.

Good for
Outdoor furniture, boats, items that may be soaked.

Not Good for
Work done where the temperature is below 70°.

Advantages
Very strong, waterproof, works well with poor joints.

Disadvantages
Powder and catalyst must be carefully mixed, has dark color.

glue and where they are best used.

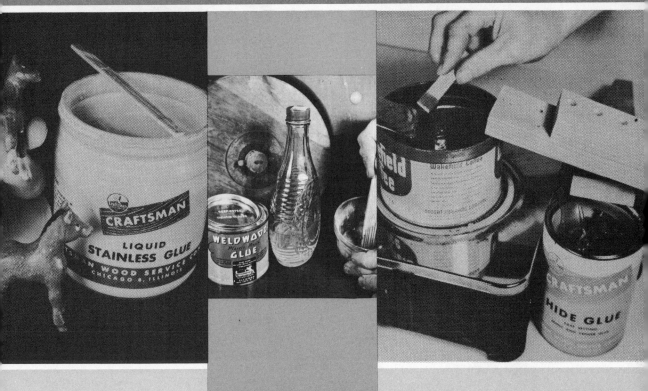

Type of Glue
White Polyvinyl
Brands include Cascorez, Wilhold, Presto-Set Glue, Elmer's Glue-all, LePage's Sure-Grip White Glue.

Good for
Model work, paper, leather, small wood assemblies, mending.

Not Good for
Anything requiring resistance to stress and water.

Advantages
Always ready to use at any temperature, non-staining.

Disadvantages
Has high cold-flow after setting; good only for light work.

Type of Glue
Plastic Resin
Brands include Weldwood, Cascamite, Formica Urea Resin Glue, LePage's Plastic Resin Glue.

Good for
Furniture, veneering, work exposed to dampness.

Not Good for
Oily woods or poorly fitted joints when clamps are not used.

Advantages
Very strong, waterproof, leaves light-colored joint.

Disadvantages
Must be mixed for each use, needs heavy clamp pressure.

Type of Glue
Flake Animal
Brands include Craftsman Hide Glue.

Good for
Quantity woodworking, furniture.

Not Good for
Anything that may be used or stored in damp places.

Advantages
Light-colored joints that need no bleaching, fills cracks and gaps in the wood.

Disadvantages
Inconvenient for quick or occasional use, must be kept hot.

How To Glue Wood

When a glue joint fails, there's a reason. But post-mortems are no substitute for durability. Check your own technique against the pointers shown here. Clamping deserves special attention—pressure should be evenly distributed and sufficient to squeeze out the excess glue but not so great as to starve the joint of adhesive by squeezing it dry.

1. If you use a powdered glue, measure it carefully if you want strong joints. There is a correct amount of water or catalyst for each powdered glue. Don't guess at the proportions. If you use flake glue, mix each ounce with 1½ ounces of water, let stand overnight and then use hot.

2. Watch the temperature when you use the glue. Animal glues won't spread when cold, and plastic-resin glues won't set properly when the temperature is below 70°. For best results with all glues, have both the glue and the work at 70° or higher.

3. Make it fit properly! No glue produces a strong joint when the fit is poor. Where you must glue a poorly fitted joint, as in repairing a loose chair rung, use an animal, casein or resorcinol glue, if possible.

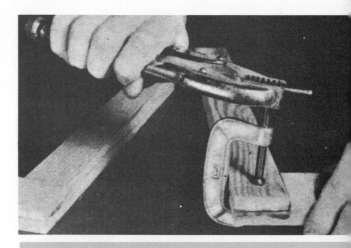

4. Clean old work thoroughly! When regluing a broken joint, scrape or sandpaper the old surface down to bare wood. Most glues work by penetrating the porous wood grain; they cannot get a grip on surfaces sealed by old glue or paint.

5. Clamp the work properly after the glue is applied. The clamp is too tight, forcing most of the glue out of the joint, and there are no blocks to spread the pressure and protect the work being glued.

6. When gluing several boards together, alternate the grain. If you glue stock edge to edge—when making a tabletop, for example—lay out the boards so that the direction of the grain alternates, presenting the heartwood side of the grain up on every other board. In the upper section of the photograph, all grain curves downward, increasing the chances that finished piece will bow later. In the lower section of the photograph, the center piece is turned with the heartwood side up, canceling out the tendency for finished piece to cup in one direction.

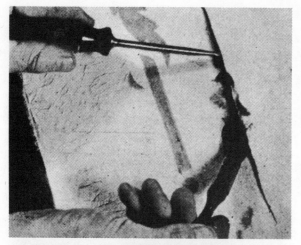

7. Apply the glue properly! Don't wear the glue brush to a frazzle using it in the wrong place, such as filling a crack. There are better ways of putting the glue where you want it. An old saw blade or even a windshield wiper does a fast job of covering broad surfaces.

8. An old photo-print roller, if you're a camera bug, can be used to spread an even layer of glue on a plywood panel, if you don't have a notched spreader or an old saw blade.

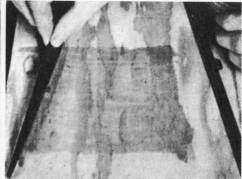

9. Chair rungs or other similar joints can be reglued without pulling them apart if a small hole is drilled into the dowel hole and the glue pumped into it with an oil can. A hypodermic needle will shoot small quantities of glue under blistered veneer or a paint-striping tool will spread it in narrow ribbons for grooves, inlay borders, cracks and other long thin work.

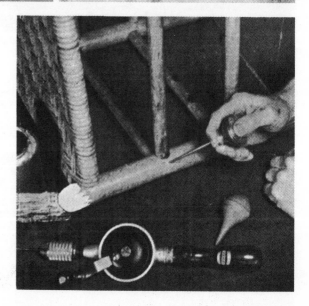

A band clamp wraps itself around curved or round work and squeezes it from all directions. You can get these clamps with either steel or heavy-canvas bands. Canvas is best for irregular shapes, steel is best suited for round or oval shapes. ▶

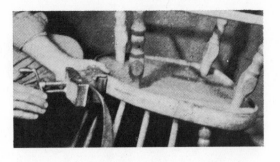

Surface clamp or bench clamp is attached to the bench top with a special bolt that fits in a T slot. When the clamp is removed, the head of the bolt slips down into a counterbored hole, leaving the bench surface clear.

There's a Clamp To Do the Job

Clamps are the craftsman's third hand. They are exceedingly handy and very necessary when working with adhesives. In addition to the clamps shown on the other pages in this section, here are a few of the special purpose clamps you will find particularly useful in your workshop.

Gluing Procedure At a Glance

Type of Glue	How To Prepare	How To Apply	Minimum Room Temperature	Setting Time at 70° Softwood—Hardwood	
Liquid animal or fish	If room is cold, warm glue to 70° or higher.	Spread on both surfaces; let get tacky before joining.	Sets best above 70° but can be used in colder room if glue is warmed.	12 hours	24 hours
Casein	Mix equal parts of glue and water. Let stand 10 minutes and stir again.	Use within 8 hours after mixing; put on a thick coat.	Any temperature above freezing, but the warmer the better.	2 hours	4 hours
Polyvinyl	Comes ready to use.	Spread on and clamp at once.	Any temperature above freezing; sets faster if warmed.	20 minutes	30 minutes
Plastic resin	Mix 2 parts of powder with ½ to 1 part of water.	Apply thin coat to one surface only.	Must be 70° or warmer. Will set faster at 90°.	4–6 hours	5–7 hours
Resorcinol	Mix 3 parts powder to 4 parts liquid catalyst.	Apply thin coat to both surfaces and clamp.	Must be 70° or warmer. Sets faster at 90°.	8 hours	10 hours
Flake or powdered animal	For each ounce of glue, add 1½ ounces of water for softwood, 2 ounces for hardwood. Keep hot and use at 140°.	Apply with a brush and work fast. It is best to warm the joint for best results.	Must be 70° or warmer. A heat lamp is useful during assembly and setting period.	12 hours	24 hours

Edge-clamp fixture attaches to short bar clamp for gluing strips to board edges. Bar clamps are screwed tightly on board, and edge clamp then applies pressure against the edge of the board. Wood strip along edge equalizes the pressure.

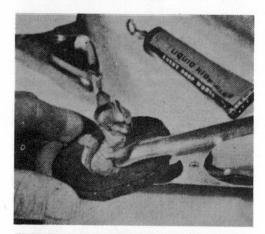

Spring clamp is best suited to light assembly work. Its chief advantage is that it can be put on with one hand while the other hand holds the parts. These overgrown clothespins are also good for small veneering jobs and border-inlay work.

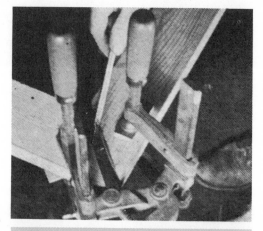

Universal clamp is a real tricky gadget. You can place it on a fitted miter joint, open the joint by twisting the center handle, apply the glue and then bring the miter tightly together again to set. It's almost like having a second pair of hands.

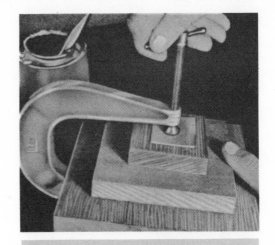

Press screw is the heart of many special gluing presses. Four or more can be made into a press for veneering panels. Here one is used to cement lineoleum to wood for making block prints. Pressure is vertical.

Deep-throated C clamps will reach into the center of small work where the pressure is most needed. These are all-metal construction and small wood pads must be used to protect the work from their jaws.

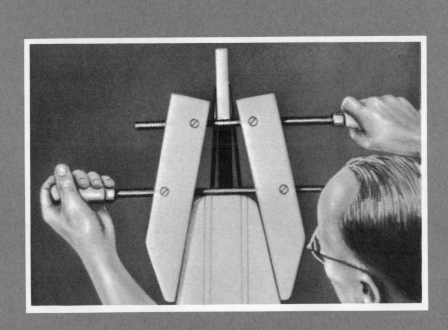

Uneven surfaces like this ironing-board end are clamped with ease with an adjustable hand screw. Screws are quickly opened or closed down to size by gripping both handles and cranking the screw in either direction.

Special Adhesives

Adhesives are used for more than the mere joining of wood to wood or metal to wood. There is a whole family of related adhesives designed for special purposes. Here are just a few of the "family;" they will be discussed more fully under their appropriate heading.

- wallpaper paste—comes ready mixed or in powder form and mixed with water; it is used to hold wallpaper to walls.
- linoleum paste and cement—generally the paste is used to hold linoleum roll goods or linoleum tiles to floors; where moisture may be encountered, linoleum cement should be used.
- asphalt tile cement—these ready-mixed adhesives should be applied with a notched trowel; a gallon usually is sufficient to cover about 144 square feet.
- rubber tile cement—care should be taken to see that this adhesive is applied without lumps; a gallon should cover about 100 square feet.
- plastic tile mastic—mastic is just a special technical name for a type of glue or adhesive; you can cover about 50 square feet of floor with one gallon of mastic.
- metal tile cement—this special adhesive covers a more limited area than the other types of special adhesives; a gallon will be enough to cover about 32 square feet.

> When applying a pressure-bonding synthetic rubber and resin adhesive (to bond a plastic laminate to plywood) use a notched spreader for an even distribution of the adhesive.

Technical Names—Trade Names

When buying an adhesive, look at the label! But too often you won't find the technical name of the glue, only the trade name. Here are the technical "family" names together with some of the trade names you will find readily available in stores:

Casein glue
   Casco, LePage's Casein Glue
Casein latex
   Casco Flexible Cement
Cellulose cement
   DuPont's Duco Cement, LePage's Miracle Mender, LePage's Liquid Solder
Hot hide glue
   Craftsman Hide Glue
Liquid fish glue
   LePage's Liquid Glue, Rogers Isinglass
Liquid hide glue
   Franklin Liquid Glue
Resorcinol resin
   Elmer's Waterproof Glue, known as Cascophen, U.S. Plywood Phenol Resorcinol Glue
Synthetic rubber and resin
  general purpose
   Goodyear's Pliobond
  pressure sensitive
   Weldwood Contact Cement, Formica Contact Cement, Roltite
Urea resin
   Weldwood, Cascamite, Formica Urea Resin Glue, LePage's Plastic Resin
White polyvinyl liquid
   Presto-set Glue, Elmer's Glue-all, LePage's Sure-Grip White Glue, Evertite Liquid Resin Glue

Photographs courtesy of Formica Company

SELECTING THE BEST ADHESIVE FOR THE JOB

WORK TO BE GLUED	GLUE TO USE
Interior woodwork, furniture, cabinetwork	*Casein* *Hot hide glue* *Liquid hide glue* *Liquid fish glue* *Urea resin* *White polyvinyl liquid*
Exterior woodwork, patio or garden furniture and any work exposed to dampness	*Casein* *Resorcinol resin glue* *Urea resin*
General household gluing	*Cellulose household cement* *Casein, flexible latex* *Liquid fish glue* *Liquid hide glue* *Synthetic rubber and resin—all purpose type* *White polyvinyl liquid*
Laminating plastics to wood or plywood	*Synthetic rubber and resin—pressure sensitive type* *Resorcinol resin glue*
Metal cabinets to tile walls, metal to wood	*Synthetic rubber and resin—all purpose type and pressure sensitive type*
Oily woods, such as teak, rosewood, yew, lemonwood	*Casein* *Resorcinol resin glue*
Furniture repairs and patching	*Casein* *Hot hide glue* *Liquid fish glue* *Liquid hide glue* *Synthetic rubber and resin* *Urea resin* *White polyvinyl liquid*

Only light pressure is necessary when using a pressure-bonding adhesive. An ordinary household rolling pin will do the job, or use any hammer and a block of wood.

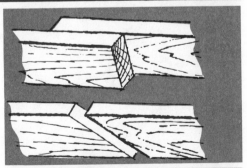

The greater the glue area, the stronger the joint. A lap joint (top) is one way to increase the glue area. The scarf joint (below) is a neater way to do the same job.

Various types of epoxies are formulated to do their best with masonry repairs. Shown here are four typical uses. Fill small holes to provide a level surface on which to lay resilient flooring; fill big cracks in concrete floors where moisture must be sealed out; use as adhesive to lay up decorative concrete block; and fill and seal small and large cracks in vertical masonry.

Photo courtesy The Woodhill Chemical Co.

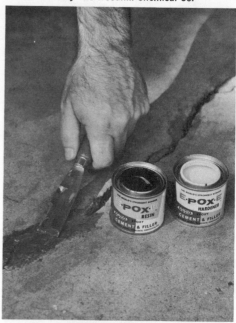

Photo courtesy Epoxy Coatings Co.

Photo courtesy Magic American Chemical Corp.

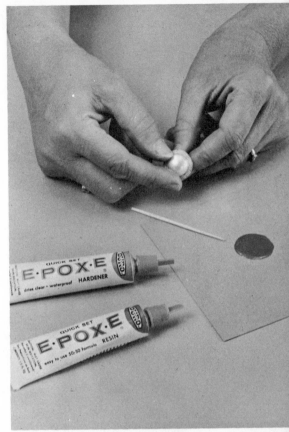

Photo courtesy The Woodhill Chemical Corp.

Photo courtesy The Woodhill Chemical Corp.

Epoxies are versatile. They are best at joining dissimilar materials, and in any joint where great strength is required. These photographs illustrate these qualities and will suggest other uses to you. Here a claw hammer is being repaired, by permanently bonding the handle to the head. A stone in a piece of costume jewelry will never work loose when epoxied. A special type of epoxy, formulated for this purpose, seals a leaky pipe joint.

THESE ARE ADHESIVES TOO

Not everything in a tube or can is an adhesive, of course, but many materials with special purposes are really in this category. Some of the products frequently used for patching cars are adhesives. For example, body putty, used to fill dents, is an adhesive of sorts. Holes in mufflers can often be patched with adhesives. Plastic Rubber, which is shown here patching worn overshoes, is an excellent all-purpose adhesive, when retention of flexibility is an important characteristic. Adhesives are also found useful in sewing—as the hem job illustrates. Your hardware store has many, many more. Next time you need an adhesive for a very special purpose, ask your dealer if he has one that will do the job.

Self-curing Plastic Rubber does repairs like these, or can be used as an all-purpose adhesive where flexibility is important.

Photo courtesy The Woodhill Chemical Co.

The magic of modern adhesives has a place in milady's sewing basket. Dabs of Fabric Mender will hold this straying hem.

Photo courtesy The Woodhill Chemical Co.

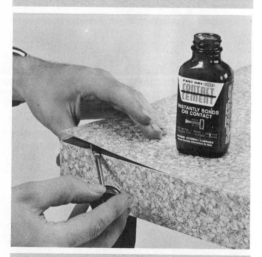

Contact cement in small bottles is useful when a piece of plastic laminate works loose from an old bond.

Photo courtesy The Woodhill Chemical Co.

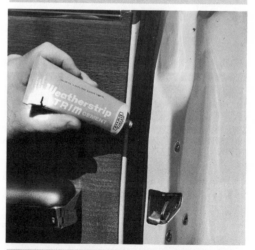

Another special purpose cement is this variety, used to refasten weatherstrip and trim around doors.

Photo courtesy The Woodhill Chemical Co.

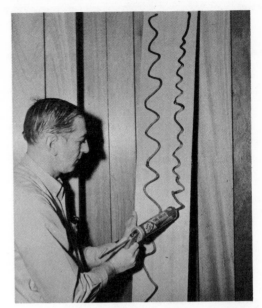

Here's a glue that does well on glass and ceramics, as its name indicates. Use it for earrings or damaged china.

Photo courtesy The Dow Corning Corp.

Random plank paneling is quickly installed with special adhesives designed for the purpose. They're applied with a gun.

Photo courtesy Sta-Tite Products Co.

Next time you have to replace a gasket on that lawnmower engine, you'll want to cement it. Golden Gasket Gloo does it.

Photo courtesy Magic American Chemical Corp.

Small dents in auto fenders can often be quickly repaired with a form of adhesive that fills in the depressions.

Photo courtesy Magic American Chemical Corp.

Chipped porcelain on a stove or other appliance is unsightly. Porcelain repair material in a squeeze tube fixes it.

Photo courtesy Magic American Chemical Corp.

Aerator

There are two types of aerators with which the home handyman should be familiar. First, there is the one used in the kitchen, and secondly, there is the one used in the garden on lawns.

The kitchen aerator is generally attached to the mixing spout of the kitchen faucets. It is there to prevent the splashing of water. The mixing of air with the water while it is running through the special unit, makes the water cling to any surface rather than "bounce off" and splash.

There are many different types of water aerators. They vary depending upon the style fixture to which they are attached. With all the special adaptors, no faucet spout or mixing spout need be without one of these splash preventors.

The second type of aerator is used by the home handyman on his lawn. The many-"tooth" unit opens up the earth to let air and water penetrate more easily.

While the homeowner with an average sized lawn has no need to buy a commercial aerator, smaller units are available. One especially useful type is attached in place of the roller bar of either a hand or power mower. Aeration is a must for a healthy lawn; for further details, see *Lawns*.

Star-spike aerator made by the Engman Co. is used in place of the roller bar of either a hand or power lawn mower.

One of the many types of water aerators that is easily attached to any faucet or spray to prevent the fast-flowing water from splashing.

Photo courtesy of P&G Supply Co.

Aggregate

Term used to describe a mixture of sand and gravel used with cement. See *Concrete*.

Air Conditioning

Photo courtesy Carrier Air Conditioning Co.

This Carrier air conditioner is unobtrusive in this room setting. Modern machines are small enough to be almost unnoticeable, while performing better than the big old units.

Air conditioning has added immeasurably to home comfort. Comfort, it seems, is achieved by an exacting combination of the right temperature with the right humidity, and neither one alone will do the trick. You can obtain this comfort in any room of your home in hot, humid weather by installing a room air conditioner. Or you can achieve greater comfort in every room by adding a home air conditioning unit.

Air conditioning does more than merely control the temperature and humidity. The better brand units also filter the air. Dust is removed, making it easier for the homemaker to keep her home clean. Irritating pollen is removed to bring relief to mil-

lions of hayfever sufferers. And today's air conditioners are exceedingly quiet. They help to cut out the outside noises and, at the same time, the motor operation of the unit itself is kept at a low noise level.

The Room Air Conditioner

Until recently, anyone adding a room air conditioner installed it at the base of the window. Depending upon the model, there was little choice—the unit would just bulge

Traditional method of installing a room air conditioner is at the base of a window. Because the unit fits flush with the window, there's no decorating problem.

Here's another "built-in" approach. A hole cut through the exterior wall of the house provides the space in any room for a modern air conditioner.

into the room and make the "window decorating" a problem. Other models projected out from the window and were an eye-sore from the exterior.

Today, you are no longer limited to the base of the window when you install air conditioning units. Furthermore, because of their more compact size and contemporary design, they blend into the room's furnishings and add to the decor instead of subtracting from it.

"Built-in" air conditioning is becoming exceedingly popular in many homes. The air conditioner is set into an exterior wall of the house and does not have to rob valuable window space. And the unit can be successfully disguised and "hidden" in the room. Even when it's not hidden, the modern styling enables it to blend in gracefully into any room's setting.

However, mounting the air conditioner in the window—whether it be at the base or along the top—is still the more common method of installing a room air conditioner. It is, by far, the simplest method of instal-

lation for the home handyman. However, if you are handy with tools and have the know-how, you can "build your air conditioner in the wall."

Home Air Conditioners

Whether you're building a new home or remodeling your existing home, you should investigate the possibility of adding a home air conditioning unit. In many cases, such a unit can be added to your existing heating system or as a supplement to it.

Here are some things to look for and questions to ask when you go to

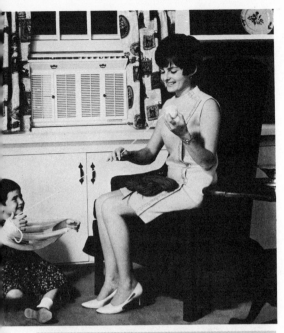

Although a modern air conditioner is attractive enough, you can disguise its presence by designing it into a wall storage unit, such as the one pictured.

Photo courtesy Carrier Air Conditioning Co.

WHERE TO PLACE A ROOM AIR CONDITIONER

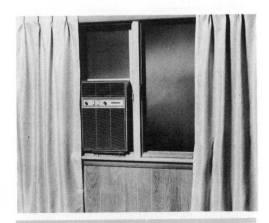

Casement windows no longer create a problem when mounting a room air conditioner. Note how easily this unit fits into the casement window, wihout cutting the metal frame.

buy your central air conditioning unit.

1. *Variety of units*—There are three basic types of units—the year-round models which heat and cool the entire home from one cabinet and are designed primarily for new houses or replacement of worn-out furnaces; the conversion units for adapting forced warm air furnaces to year-round air conditioning; and the summer air conditioning units which are installed independently of the heating system.

2. *Survey and estimate*—A home air conditioning unit is not one for the average home handyman to install himself. He should secure the services of a reliable dealer. A good dealer will visit your home, draw a rough floor plan and estimate the cooling load needed for your home. He cannot tell you how much it will cost over the telephone.

3. *Humidity control*—An air conditioner's cooling coil lowers temperature and reduces humidity simultaneously. However, some systems will adequately control temperature but will not control humidity. Although the amount of surface of the cooling coil influences this, the basic factors in good humidity control are proper sizing of the unit and design of the system. When the air conditioner is too large for the amount of heat to be removed, it will turn itself off a good portion of the time and moisture will reevaporate from the cooling coil. When you're shopping for comfort, this is an important point to check with your dealer.

4. *Sturdy construction*—A central air conditioner should be expected to last a good long time and this requires sturdy construction of

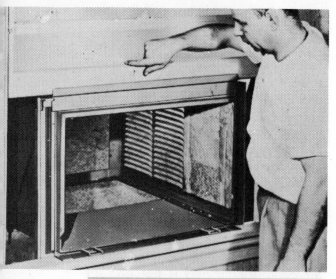

1. Place the cabinet so that it's centered in the window frame. Lower the bottom sash so that it holds the cabinet in place.

3. Secure the "L" brackets with screws and slide expandable wings against window frame. Tighten screws to lock wings to brackets.

HOW TO INSTALL A ROOM AIR CONDITIONER

2. Open partially the expandable wings and slide the "L" brackets into position on each side of the cabinet resting in the window.

the cabinet as well as of other parts. While you can't be expected to tell the gage of the steel without a micrometer, a few taps on the cabinet can reassure you that it's of solid manufacture.

5. *Insulation*—The air conditioner's cabinet should be heavily insulated against sound and heat transmission. Look inside the unit. Certain portions of the ductwork which are exposed to non-air-conditioning space should also be insulated.

6. *Water use*—Some central air conditioners use water for refrigerant condensing and others have been developed which require no water at all. The reason is that some communities

Photos courtesy of Mitchell Manufacturing Co.

have legislated against water consumption for air conditioning. In other areas, water is simply in short supply, expensive, or difficult to dispose of, or may become so in some easily foreseeable future time. One air conditioned home on a block may not present much of a strain on the available water supply, but a dozen might. The best way to decide which type of unit you should obtain is to check with your local water supply company or city department as well as the dealer.

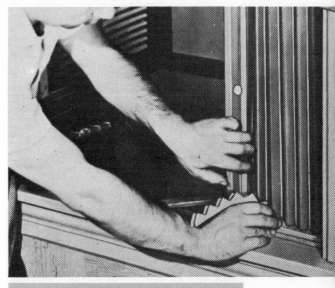

4. Cut sawtooth sponge rubber inserts to required length and insert them between the expandable wing panels and window sill.

5. Insert the air conditioner chassis, sliding it forward into the completely assembled cabinet that's been secured in window.

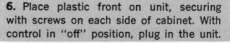

6. Place plastic front on unit, securing with screws on each side of cabinet. With control in "off" position, plug in the unit.

The "New Look" with Air Conditioned Homes

An extensive recent survey indicates that changes, both interior and exterior, are beginning to appear in homes designed around air conditioning.

The most obvious exterior design changes are related to turning back the heat of the sun. More roofs are being painted white and roof overhangs are being extended to protect window's from the sun's glare. Orientation of windows is getting more attention from builders and architects.

Indoors, the changes are most apparent in terms of greater convenience. For example, take the bedroom which is usually difficult to furnish because it requires so much furniture in such a small space. In addition, walls are frequently broken up by standard double-hung windows necessary to provide good ventilation. With air conditioning, windows can be moved up on the wall to give greater privacy as well as more wall space for furniture.

Similar changes can be found in living areas. Imagine a living-room with a wall entirely of glass facing south—an exposure which can be satisfactorily shielded from the sun by roof overhang. Another wall without windows faces west where the afternoon heat of the sun through glass would be intense. This solid wall can now be used for built-ins or a convenient furniture arrangement.

The kitchen is the hottest room in the home and ordinarily needs a good deal of cross-ventilation. But scattering windows around the walls plays havoc with efficient arrangement of cabinets and working space.

Since air conditioning makes cross-ventilation unnecessary, bedroom windows can be set high in the wall and furniture placed underneath.

Windows need no longer break up an efficient kitchen cabinet arrangement. They can be paced over the sink where most housewives like them, leaving the other walls solid.

With air conditioning cross-ventilation is no longer necessary and the window area can be confined to one wall. An exhaust fan over the range takes away cooking odors.

Air conditioning can also recover what might once have been considered virtually unusable space, and permit its use on the same basis as other areas of the house. This is particularly true of the basement, where dampness, mildew, rust and dirt have frequently hampered its full use as a hobby, recreation, activity or even storage area. But an air conditioned basement properly protected against leakage of water from outside can become a completely enjoyable part of the home.

In many homes, solid walls can be used on some exposures, providing valuable space for built-ins, and other exposures can be entirely of glass for view and light.

Decorating colors can be lighter if the room is air conditioned, since much of the normal grime and dirt are eliminated.

Air conditioning can make basements as livable as any other portion of the house. Year-round air conditioning reduces humidity, thus cutting mildew and rust, and filters dust and dirt from the air it circulates.

Selecting the Size of a
Room Air Conditioner

The following simple method of determining the proper size air conditioner for a room is suggested by Carrier Corporation. It requires only four calculations to arrive at the total cooling units required. Simply fill in the figures requested below, multiply by the special multiplier and place the answer in the right hand column. When finished, add up the right hand column and the job is done. Residential windows are based on an average of 12 square feet each.

1. Windows
Count the number of windows on which the sun shines at any time during the day and enter the total here.

_____ × 500 = _____

Count the number of windows which face north or are in the shade all day and enter the total here.

_____ × 250 = _____

2. Floor Area
Compute the number of square feet of floor area of the space to be cooled and enter the total here.

_____ × 30 = _____

3. Uninsulated Roof
If the space to be cooled is under an uninsulated roof exposed to the sun, enter the same square footage as above.

_____ × 9 = _____

To select the proper size unit, add all the totals and consult the following table.

Up to 4,700 Cooling Units requires a 1/3 HP unit.
4,800 to 7,100 Cooling Units requires a 1/2 HP unit.
7,200 to 11,100 Cooling Units requires a 3/4 HP unit.
11,200 to 14,200 Cooling Units requires a 1 HP unit.
14,300 to 20,000 Cooling Units requires a 1 1/2 HP unit.

Adding Central Air Conditioning to the Home

Economical air conditioning of any kind of house is now possible with the introduction of new central air conditioning equipment. The last large category of existing homes previously considered difficult or expensive to air condition—those with hot water or steam heat and those without central heating systems—can now add summer cooling at a reasonable cost without modifying the heating equipment.

Practically all homes fall into one of the following five categories as far as heating systems are concerned.

plications, you can install a summer air conditioner such as the Summer Weathermaker. The small unit located inside the house contains cooling and dehumidifying coils, filter and air-circulation fan. It can be hung from the ceiling in a hallway, closet or utility room, or placed in a minimum space in the attic, basement or crawl space.

The simplest kind of duct system can be used because perimeter discharge of air which is usually advisable for heating systems in cool climates is not necessary for cooling. It is connected to a refrigerating unit requiring no water which is located outside.

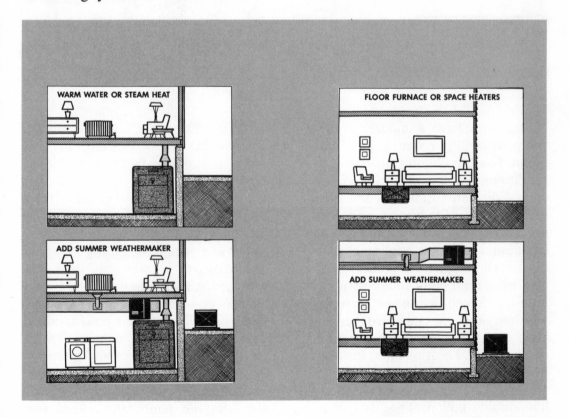

1. If you live in a home with warm water or steam heat using radiators or one of the other radiant heat ap-

2. If your house has a floor furnace or space heaters, the approach is the same as for houses with wet heat.

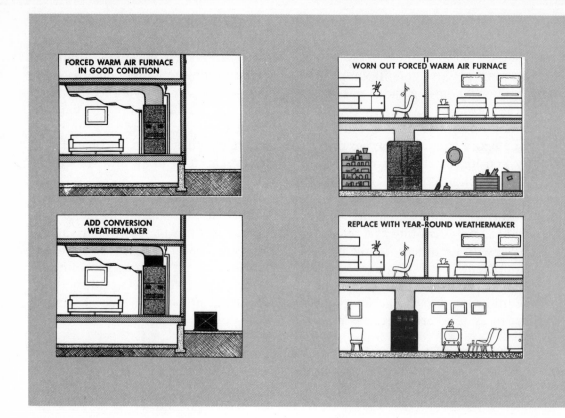

FORCED WARM AIR FURNACE IN GOOD CONDITION

ADD CONVERSION WEATHERMAKER

WORN OUT FORCED WARM AIR FURNACE

REPLACE WITH YEAR-ROUND WEATHERMAKER

3. If you have a modern forced warm air heating system in good condition, you can obtain year-round air conditioning at a comparatively low cost. You can install a conversion unit which uses the furnace and existing duct system for filtering and air circulation and adds cooling and dehumidifying. There are models available which can be installed with any kind of forced warm air furnace, whether, it is the standard vertical type, counterflow or down-flow unit, or a horizontal heating plant installed in a crawl space or attic.

The small, quiet cooling and dehumidifying coil package is located at the discharge end of the furnace, and a weatherproof and tamperproof refrigerating unit requiring no water is placed out of doors.

4. If you have a forced warm air furnace which is getting old and worn, it might be better to replace it with a summer and winter unit like the Year-Round Weathermaker than to try to convert it. You can usually use the same duct system. This is less expensive than installing a new forced warm air unit and adding a conversion unit later on.

The complete unit handles both summer and winter air conditioning. It supplies cooling, dehumidifying, heating, air circulation and filtering. A simple control shifts it from cooling to heating and the same thermostat sets the temperature level for summer and winter. It is available either with air-cooled refrigeration using no water, or water-cooled, and for heating it burns oil or gas.

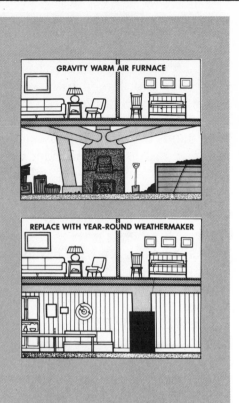

GRAVITY WARM AIR FURNACE

REPLACE WITH YEAR-ROUND WEATHERMAKER

The conversion unit pictured below adapts a warm air heating system to year-round air conditioning. It is placed in the basement and used with a standard vertical furnace.

5. If you have an old gravity warm air furnace with warm air pipes coming off in all directions, your best bet is to replace it completely with a unit which will provide winter and summer air conditioning. Conversion is not recommended. Some modification will be necessary in the ducts and outlets, but you would need this if you installed a new forced warm air system.

This conversion unit, designed for a down-flow forced warm air furnace, is shown installed in a first floor closet of a house with no basement. The furnace is lifted a few inches to allow the small counterflow coil to go underneath.

Placing a Home Air Conditioner

Although central air conditioners can be installed in a basement, there are other locations in the house which can be used if there is no basement space available.

*Photographs and sketches courtesy of
Carrier Corporation*

Here the conversion unit is added to a horizontal forced warm air furnace, installed in the crawl space of a house with no basement.

Alkyd

This is a classification of paints which has alkyd resins instead of oils as a base. The label on the can may read "glycerol phthalate resin," a term which is synonymous with alkyd resin.

Alkyd resins paints are considered superior in wearing quality to the older oil base paints. Among the advantages claimed for this type of paint are: it's tougher, it resists fading better than the oil base types, it will not yellow and it can be washed easily and safely. Furthermore, alkyd base paints dry fairly rapidly and do not have the disagreeable odor characteristic of many of the oil base paints.

Also see *PAINTS*.

Allen Screw

Setscrews or cap screws which have a hexagonal socket in the head are called Allen screws. They are adjusted by means of a hexagonal key or wrench, commonly called an Allen wrench.

See *ALLEN WRENCH*.

Allen Wrench

Used with Allen screws, the wrenches are available in several different styles. Actually, the Allen screw is more like a bolt than the conventional wood or sheet metal screw. The top, instead of being a slot, is a six-sided hole into which the Allen wrench fits.

Allen wrenches come in different sizes to match the individual Allen screws, which are commonly used to keep metal parts together. For example, the sliding arm of a circle cutter is secured by an Allen screw as are the blades in most better-made power jig saws.

The Allen wrench is usually a tool's "tool." It is used to tighten or loosen Allen screws, which hold metal parts together.

Here are two of the more popular types of Allen wrenches. Left: combination wrench with a series of different sized Allen wrenches. Right: examples of L-shaped wrenches.

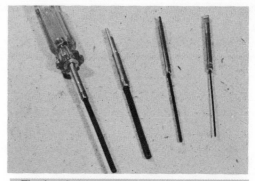

The handyman who has many power tools or is active in metal working will find this socket handle with interchangeable wrenches a valuable addition to his workshop.

Alligator Clips

These serrated-edged clips are used on ends of test wires. While most frequently used with radio and TV wires for temporary hook-ups, they can also be used on electrical test boards to test bell, battery and electric train wiring if any failure arises.

While alligator clips can also be used for testing of normal household electric lines, the average handyman should avoid these open contacts. The more advanced handyman, while using these clips, should make certain that he uses the type with insulated hold-ends and that he does not come into contact with the exposed ends while the current is on.

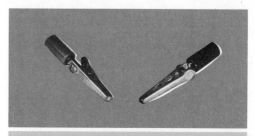

Alligator clips for test wires.

Alligatoring

This is the term used to describe the cracking of a painted surface. The surface resembles the hide of an alligator. It is most commonly caused by the application of a thick layer of paint over a recently painted surface which has not become thoroughly hard and dry. When this defect in a painted surface occurs, it is necessary to sand or scrape the surface smooth before repainting or remove the old paint.

Also see *PAINTING*.

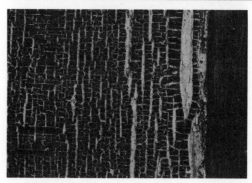

Photograph courtesy of Pittsburgh Plate Glass Co.

Aluminum

Aluminum is impervious to rust, rot, vermin and is one of the few metals with a long life independent of special processing or frequent painting. With the development of the new alloy, *Do-It-Yourself Aluminum* has opened new fields to the home craftsman. New uses are being devised every day and it has become a stock item in the home craftsman's workshop.

Do-It-Yourself Aluminum comes in a great variety of shapes and sizes including plain and embossed sheets, tubing, rod, angle, bar and clear plastic sheet. Aluminum hardware consists of corner locks, screen and storm sash hanging devices, machine screws, wood screws, sheet metal screws and rivets.

Special extruded shapes are available for storm sash and screen frame members featuring aluminum splines for screen or sheet plastic storm sash construction. Rain gutters and downspouts as well as the hardware to mount them are stock items.

Many finishes and textures can be given to the aluminum surface by grinding, polishing, scratch brushing, buffing, burnishing, tumbling, highlighting, fluting, sandblasting, embossing and spin finishing. Paints, enamels, varnishes and lacquers can also be used after the surface is cleaned for proper bonding.

Tools for Working with Do-It-Yourself Aluminum

The new Do-It-Yourself Aluminum is softer than tool steel so that the ordinary hand and power tools in your workshop can be used safely and efficiently on this material.

Cutting and Marking Hints

1. To mark sheet aluminum use the flat steel square to check corners and mark accurately and clearly.

2. Circles and arcs on small projects can be marked with a pencil compass and a sharp pencil or scriber. Avoid scribing too deeply.

3. Avoid confusion and mistakes when marking aluminum surfaces by using dots in a circle, V marks or crossed lines to indicate measured and cutting areas.

4. Make a simple mitre box from scrap or plywood to cut rods or tubes at an angle.

5. Use wood blocks with V channels cut in them to protect aluminum surfaces of rods and tubes held in vise jaws.

6. The use of oil or paraffin will reduce friction, chatter and give greater efficiency and accuracy in cutting aluminum.

7. Adhesive, friction or marking tape carefully wound around tubing or rods will serve as a guide line for accurate right angle cuts.

Marking Tools

Marking tools are probably the first tools which you will use to plan your layouts and designs. A scratch awl, a pair of dividers, a steel rule, a pencil, crayon or sharp nail may be used for marking the aluminum. Avoid scribing too deeply.

A flat steel square will work better than the combination wood and metal square because it will be in full contact with the working surface and will contribute to greater accuracy. Always tip on edge any thick measuring devices such as yardsticks or zigzag rules to get accurate pin point measurements.

Cutting Tools

Cutting tools for your aluminum projects will depend upon the thickness and shape of the stock you are using.

For tubes, rods, bars and extruded shapes, a good wood saw or hacksaw will do. The more teeth per inch on the saw blade the finer and neater the cut.

Irregular curved lines can be cut

Ordinary kitchen shears shown above can cut through sheet aluminum.

with precision and fine edges with a coping, scroll or jeweler's saw.

A pocket knife will remove burrs from inside tubes and can be used for small interior cuts on the plain and embossed sheets.

An ordinary pair of household scissors or combination tin snips will cut the plain and embossed sheet aluminum easily and accurately.

Small interior areas can be cut cleanly and neatly with a sharp cold chisel or a wood chisel. The metal should be laid over a piece of smooth scrap wood to save the tool edge when using a wood chisel. Long-toothed single-cut files which do not clog up are effective cutting tools. A file card or steel brush will keep the teeth clean.

Auger bits in a carpenter's brace or a hand drill with twist drills will cut screw, rivet and larger holes. All sheets must be backed with scrap wood for neat, clean holes. Drilling accuracy in sheet, bar, tube or angle stock will be guaranteed if you use a center punch or nail tapped lightly to give the bit a resting place.

Regular wood handsaws work well in cutting Do-It-Yourself Aluminum. Fine-toothed saws are recommended. Lubricate saw with paraffin for smooth cuts.

Photographs courtesy of Reynolds Metals Co.

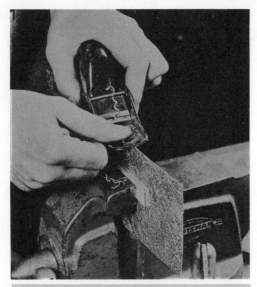

A wood working block plane may be used for smoothing or trimming edges. Use a light cut for best results.

Your regular wood planes are suitable for dressing down the aluminum stock of sheet, bar or angle material. Always make a light cut and repeat cuts to get greater depth of cut.

A wood expansion bit backed up with smooth scrap wood will cut the large holes efficiently and cleanly in sheet stock.

Forming Tools and Jigs

Various hammers and mallets are useful in bending and forming aluminum sheet metal, bars, and angle stock. Plastic tipped, rubber, wood and rawhide mallets will prevent marring and marking your projects. A light ball peen hammer will do double duty in clinching rivets, forming shallow trays and coasters and in planishing. Planishing is the name given to the process of making a hammered and dimpled effect on metal with a ball peen hammer or other shaped hammer.

Pliers and wrenches used for holding and twisting the metal should have their jaws padded with tape to prevent marring. Wooden and metal jigs for bending, forming and holding the metal stock are described in more detail in the section on Forming and Fastening Aluminum.

Your regular selection of screwdrivers and wrenches will take care of the screws, nuts and bolts which will be used on your projects.

Power Tools

BENCH SAW—A bench saw with any of the following accessories will take care of all cuts necessary in your projects; regular wood or metal blades, i.e., combination, rip or crosscut, emery wheel used on saw and sanding discs.

When feeding your aluminum stock into the blade on a bench saw the work may tend to rise up from the saw. This can be overcome by making a wood plate from a small

A wood expansion bit bores clean holes through the Do-It-Yourself sheet aluminum. Back-up the sheet metal with a smooth wood block as shown above.

section of plywood and clamping or screwing it to the saw fence.

The blade should be permitted to cut into the wood plate. This jig will not only eliminate the metal's tendency to climb, but it will also protect you from flying metal chips.

BAND SAW AND JIG SAW—The band saw used with the standard wood blades or metal cutting blades plus a back-up board for stack cutting will give neat, accurate results. A thin sheet of wood under the aluminum stock when jig-sawing will prevent chatter, binding and ragged edges. Your jig-saw can be used with the regular blades, with metal cutting blades or the jig-saw file set.

DRILL PRESS—The drill press can be used with twist drills, wood bits or circular cutters as well as to buff and polish your finished projects. To use auger bits in the drill press grind the lead screw to a point. Power wood bits will cut aluminum more effectively if a pilot hole is drilled first to receive the tip of the bit.

Carefully center punch all holes before drilling and be sure to clamp

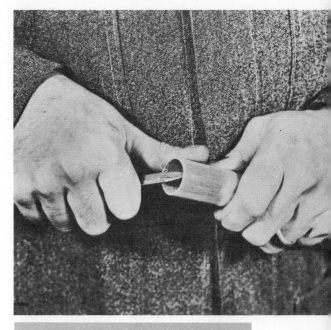

An ordinary pocket knife as shown above will cut and trim aluminum. Burrs are easily removed from tubes, bars, rods and angle metal.

your work to the press table with a smooth piece of scrap wood underneath.

The sunswirl effect seen on compacts, cigarette cases is also a decorative device you can make on your aluminum projects with the drill press or hand power tool.

To make the sunswirl tool, cement a soft disc of rubber to the end of a ½" dowel and glue a circular piece of emery cloth to the rubber pad. Chuck the dowel in the press and run it slowly while raising and lowering the press handle.

Buffing and polishing on aluminum projects can be done on the drill press as well as with a portable power drill.

JOINTER—Used with the standard blades your jointer will dress down the longer pieces of angle and bar aluminum stock. As with the

A coping, scroll or jeweler's saw will cut mitre corners as well as curves, scrolls and designs in the aluminum stock.

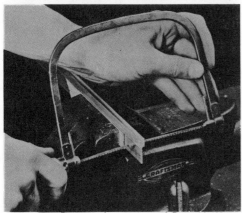

Photographs courtesy of Reynolds Metals

hand plane, set the blades for a shallow cut and use oil or paraffin on the metal surfaces to reduce drag.

Forming Do-It-Yourself Aluminum

Any mallet that's smooth and soft such as plastic, rubber, wood or rawhide will provide a good neat working surface. To bend sheet metal lay it over the edge of a smooth board and gently mallet it to the angle desired.

A sheet bending jig for special projects may be made by sawing a slot or groove lengthwise into a piece of wood with a bench saw. The slot or groove is cut to the depth of the required bend or brake.

A simple jig can be fashioned from two boards clamped to either side of the metal at the proper depth while another board or mallet is used to turn the metal over. A section of angle iron or aluminum clamped to the smooth sharp edge of a board or work bench will hold the sheet firmly for malleting.

To roll edges, saw a slot lengthwise in a dowel, broom handle, pipe or any cylindrical object of desired size. Insert the sheet in the slot and wrap around by hand.

Shallow ash trays and coasters can be formed from discs of sheet metal by using the end grain of a block of wood clamped in a vise as a back-up and tapping the metal gently with a hammer in a circular motion. The disc must be kept at a constant angle until the metal has been tapped in a complete circle. Hammering cold metal will make it hard and brittle, so practice on some scraps before you tackle your job.

Bending solid rods, bars, and tubes can be accomplished in a vise with various hand tools and with simple jigs which you can make from scrap wood in a few minutes. To use your metal-working vise on aluminum projects, cover the jaws of the vise with scraps of aluminum to prevent marring and chewing of the material you are working.

To make 45° or 90° angles with bar or rod stock, clamp the metal parallel to the vise jaws and push the extended end of the material with one hand while striking the metal near the vise with a mallet. A block of wood with a hole drilled through it slightly larger than the rod stock makes a good bending jig.

Bar stock can also be bent in a wood block which has had a notch cut into it and secured in a vise. Use a mallet to get sharp bends.

A round wooden jig cut from scrap

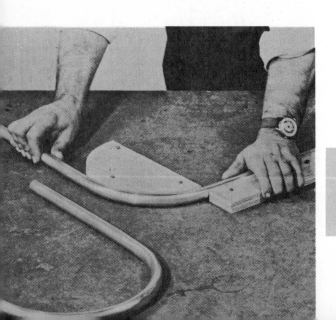

Simple jigs made from plywood or scrap blocks and boards are used to bend your aluminum stock in a variety of shapes and sizes.

Photograph courtesy of Reynolds Metals

The smallest radius to which it is possible to bend the various diameter tubes filled with sand are:

DIAMETER OF TUBE	SMALLEST RADIUS
¾"	2½"
1"	4¾"
1¾"	5½"

plywood with a notch in it, anchored to the bench, will form circles and curves.

Twists for furniture legs and decorative effects are made by fastening one end of an aluminum bar in the vise, covering the bar with a length of pipe and then twisting with a wrench or pliers at the free end of the bar. The length of pipe over the bar stock will hold the aluminum straight while the twists are forming.

An exact square corner on the inside of a bar bend is formed by sawing a small slot in the exact position where the bar is to be bent.

Jigs for forming tubes, rods and bars in curves are cut from scrap boards or plywood. Draw your pattern on the wood and remove the excess wood with a jig-saw or coping saw. On a level, rigid surface, fasten the pattern with nails, screws or bolts. At a distance equal to the thickness of the stock being formed and at the beginning of the curve fasten a small block of wood as an anchor point in your jig. Be sure the anchor block is located at the beginning of the curve. Insert your stock between the anchor block and the curved jig and slowly bend.

Sharp curves in aluminum tubes can be made without buckling the walls if you fill the tubes with damp sand before bending. To do this, insert a wooden stopper in one end of the aluminum tubing, then take a bucket of wet sand and push the tube into the bucket, tamping with the tube until it is firmly packed with sand. Form the curves and bends very slowly in your jig. This operation must be done slowly and carefully because, in bending a tube, the metal on the outside wall of the tube is being stretched while the metal on the inner wall of the tube is being compressed. Bending too fast will result in buckling on the inner wall, rupturing on the outer wall, flattening or all three.

If you must bend without using sand packed in the aluminum tube, double the suggested radius in the table above.

A free-hand method of bending tubes and rods is to place smooth dowels in a block of wood, two steel pins in a block of steel or two bolts in a vise, slightly farther apart than the thickness of the stock, and pull slowly and steadily on the free end of the stock.

Angle stock for special projects can be formed from strips of sheet metal in a vise or bending jig. Angle aluminum can be bent by drilling a hole at the point where the bend is to be made and cutting away a wedge of metal to the angle desired. The bend is then formed around a length of rod or dowel of the proper size.

Mitred corners in angle stock can be formed by cutting away a wedge of metal on one leg of the angle stock and bending in a vise with the help of a mallet.

Fastening Do-It-Yourself Aluminum

There are a number of ways to join the different shapes and sizes of aluminum stock using rivets, clips, tabs and slots, grooved seams, screws and nuts and bolts.

RIVETS—First choose the proper size drill to make the hole for the rivets. The shank of the drill should match the body of the rivet for a good tight fit. The proper length for the rivet to hold properly and firmly should be approximately one and one half times the thickness of the rivet.

Insert the rivet into the drilled holes and make sure that the sheets being joined are drawn together. Back-up the rivet with a piece of steel and with the ball end of your ball peen hammer, mushroom the end of the rivet. Follow this procedure until you have completed joining the sheets. Smooth all rivet ends with a power tool, fine sandpaper or emery cloth.

TABS AND SLOTS—Mechanical interlocking of various pieces in

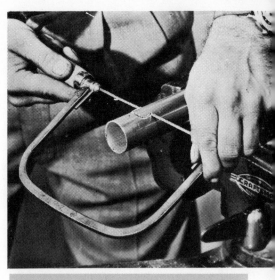

All types of joints and fastenings are possible with this type of aluminum. Shown above a coping saw is used to cut an opening in aluminum tubing for a right angle joint made with two different diameter tubes.

an aluminum project can be accomplished by cutting the tabs and slots carefully with a ¼″ wood chisel. If you go through Junior's toy box you will find a good many of his toys joined in this fashion and you can see how it is done.

GROOVED SEAM—The simplest method of joining two pieces of sheet metal is the grooved seam. To do this, first fold over the corresponding edges an equal amount, hook the lips together then with a mallet and block of wood, hammer them together. A few dimples along the seam made with a hammer and center punch or nail will prevent the seam from working loose.

In working on some of your projects, you may find it necessary to join a bar to a rod with a rivet. Your joint will be simple and strong if you form a shoulder on the rod by sawing or filing a flat surface on the rod then joining the two pieces and drilling a hole for the rivet.

The procedure just mentioned is followed to make a swivel joint on two rods, except that both rods are filed flat and then drilled and riveted.

Angles can be joined to metal sheets with self-tapping screws, sheet metal screws or in some cases nuts and bolts.

There are a number of methods of joining sheet metal to tubes. One is to slit the tube lengthwise, insert the sheet metal into the slot and secure with a sheet metal or self-tapping screw. The sheet metal can also be kept firmly in position by inserting dowel rods into either end of the tubing.

Tubing can be used for a leg or stand by making four flaps in the end of the tube, bending them over and placing screws through the flaps into the piece of wood or metal to be supported.

Corner gussets can be used to join angles or bars with rivets or nuts and bolts. When you bend a piece of angle aluminum to make a corner, the wedge of metal cut from the angle leg can be used as the reinforcing gusset for that corner.

When it is necessary to join two ends of a bar as in trimming counter tops a dovetail joint will hold firmly and neatly. Mark the joint carefully and accurately with a scratch awl, then cut with a saw on the inside of your markings, then carefully file away excess metal for a perfect, tight joint.

A hinge may easily be cut and bent, using a piece of wire coat hanger for the hinge pin. Many intricate designs and antique hinges can be easily made of aluminum for any of your projects. When measuring the tab allowance, mark off 3½ times the diameter of the wire on each side. Always make an odd number of sections to equalize the strain.

In many cases, for decorative effects, you may wish to join two sections of sheet metal together with a clip. To make this joint, bend back both edges an equal amount, from another piece of metal form a clip by determining the amount of bend necessary to draw the two sheets firmly together. Force the clip onto the bent sheet edges with a mallet, level and tighten the clip by malleting over with a smooth block of wood and dimple with a nail or center punch for added strength.

A favorite woodworker's joint, the cross-lap, can also be utilized with Do-It-Yourself aluminum bars and rods. Here again as with the dovetail joint extreme care is necessary for an accurate joint. Mark the pieces with a scratch awl, saw inside the awl marks and finish with a file, checking frequently for a proper fit.

A bench saw with a combination, rip or cross-cut blade will cut through this soft aluminum stock.

Photographs courtesy of Reynolds Metals

Aluminum tubes can be joined to many flat surfaces such as wood, angle metal, sheet metal, bars and other material by squeezing the end of the tube flat in a vise and drilling for screw holes. Tubes can be joined to wood for legs by using the above method or by inserting a section of wood dowel in the end of the tube and running a screw through the tube, dowel and into the wood. Tubes can be lengthened by inserting a plug part way into one end of the tube and forcing another section of tubing over the wood plug. Screws can be driven into the tube section to give added strength.

A "T" joint or other butt joint can be made with aluminum tubing if the tube end is fitted with a dowel. This tube end is then marked and cut with a scroll saw and a half-round file to the outside dimensions of the tube it will be joined to. A long wood screw is then driven through the tubes for a long-lasting tight joint. A variety of joints and fastenings can be devised for the Do-It-Yourself Aluminum. You will find that as you begin to work with this metal you will develop special joints and fastenings to suit the particular projects you are working on. There are also special elbows, T-butt and flanges available, made of aluminum, to fit all sizes of tubes.

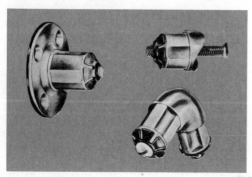

Polishing and Finishing

Very fortunately aluminum is one of the few metals which can be polished and finished in a number of different and decorative fashions without getting involved in any long and laborious operations. Various degrees of fineness in the different types of abrasives you use will give you the different effects in the buffing and finishing process.

The most common abrasive materials available to you are steelwool, fine grades of sandpaper, emery cloth, pumice stone and in an emergency tooth powder. The finer the abrasive, the brighter the finish.

Scratchbrush and satin finishes are obtained by using steelwool of varying grades or different types of wire wheels. The wheels are made of different metals in degrees of fineness. The finer the wire, the smoother the texture of the finish.

A process called planishing, light hammering with a ball peen hammer, will produce an interesting effect on bars, rods and sheet metal. Rubbing the surface of the metal after the planishing will produce a soft satin two-toned effect. To secure the best effects, you must planish on a hard surface, preferably a block of hardwood.

In addition to the planishing, a variety of decorative patterns can be developed by filing and pointing nails in different shapes and using them to tap designs on the metal surfaces. Innumerable designs and patterns can be etched into the surface of the aluminum with acids.

To etch a pattern, the portions of the design to remain shiny are blocked out by coating them over with turpentine-base asphaltum varnish, using turpentine as a solvent. A heavy creamy solution of black stove polish can be used if asphaltum is unavailable. Two coats of the blocking material are usually necessary to prevent spotting and to assure proper coverage.

A 50% solution of muriatic acid and water will make a strong enough etching solution. *Be sure, when mixing the acid bath, to pour the acid into the water. Never pour water into acid! Wear an apron and rubber gloves. Cover the work surface and surrounding area with several thicknesses of newspapers or wrapping paper. Avoid contact with bare hands or clothing. The solution must be mixed in glass or crockery; never use any metal containers. The regular household lye can be substituted if the acid is not available.*

Draw your design on paper or tracing paper and transfer the design with carbon paper to the metal surface. Paint the blocking solution over those surfaces and design portions which you want to remain shiny. Place the metal to be etched in a deep glass dish or glass tray and cover the metal surface with the acid bath. Let the metal remain in the solution until the boiling ceases, usually fifteen minutes to an hour. Pour off the solution, and examine your pattern. A second application of acid bath may be necessary if a deeper bite is desired.

After the acid solution bath, rinse with water and remove the blocking paint with turpentine, kerosene, benzine or white gasoline. Use a soft cloth to prevent marring and scratching on the polished surfaces. *Be sure*

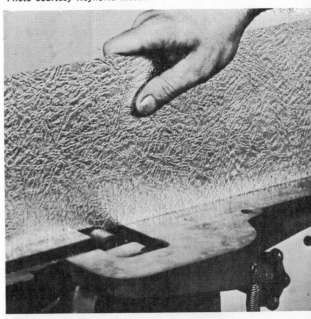

A sheet of embossed aluminum is shown being trimmed down on a jointer. Make shallow cuts and oil the metal surfaces to prevent binding.

that you have taken the necessary fire precaution steps when removing the blocking.

The final step is to wash with hot soapy water and dry. The highlight areas can be polished with 000 steel-wool and powdered pumice for a high lustrous finish.

Projects made of aluminum can be painted, enameled, varnished or lacquered with excellent results. The aluminum surface to be covered must be prepared by cleaning with steel-wool, fine sandpaper, lacquer thinner or hot soapy water. A wash with vinegar and a rinse with clear water will also remove surface oils and dirt.

Once the surface is cleaned, do not touch the metal with the hands. Natural oils from the skin will adhere to the metal and prevent proper bonding of the covering paint.

Embossed sheet aluminum can be given a coat of paint or lacquer and after the surface covering has dried a careful rubbing of the raised metal surfaces will leave the pigment in the depressed portion of the design to produce a leathery or antique finish. Steelwool carefully manipulated will do a fast clean job for you.

A bright finish on your polished projects can be maintained easily by using auto wax and buffing to a high lustre.

Helpful Hints

On all of your aluminum projects, use only aluminum nails, screws and other hardware made of aluminum. If these materials aren't available, then use chrome- or cadmium-plated hardware to avoid an unsightly rust or corrosion.

Before you tackle any original designs or ideas, draw and lay out the project on heavy paper or light cardboard. The paper or cardboard can be bent or folded to follow your design. In this way you will avoid wasting any metal and can make corrections before a single piece of metal is measured and cut. In addition, the corrected test pattern can then be used to lay out your project on the metal to scale.

When you file sheet edges or other thin pieces of metal, move your file as nearly parallel to the edge of the metal as possible. This method will give you long clean cuts, your file won't chatter and bind and your strokes will give you a continuous even surface.

The best way to find out about aluminum is to get a supply of the metal and work on some small projects first to get the feel of the metal and your tools. The small one-night projects illustrated will give you practice in cutting, bending and finishing aluminum.

A series of plans are illustrated to give you directions in cutting, assembling various simple but attractive pieces of furniture. You will find as you progress from one project to another that you will be incorporating many of your own ideas into these projects and that eventually you will be tailoring aluminum projects to your own specific needs.

One Night Aluminum Projects for the Handyman

Photographs courtesy of Reynolds Metals

Here are a few suggestions for one night projects to help you become acquainted with cutting and bending the soft variety of aluminum. After you have completed a few of these projects you will find that many new designs and ideas will suggest themselves to you.

Wall Primitives can be cut from embossed aluminum.

Simple cutting, bending, and finishing operations produce these decorative items from sheet aluminum.

This handsome fireplace set is simple to make from Do-It-Your-self Aluminum.

There is no limit to the variety of party decorations that you can make.

Try making one of these fascinating "mobiles" for a Christmas decoration.

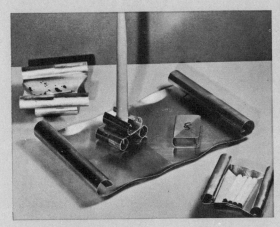

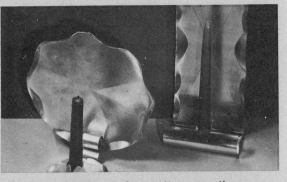

The attractive surface patterns on these two candlestick holders and reflectors are produced by masking off sections separately and sandpapering them lightly or rubbing with steel wool.

An attractive desk set can be made easily and quickly.

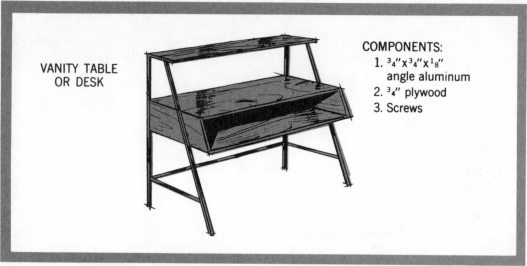

VANITY TABLE
OR DESK

COMPONENTS:
1. $\frac{3}{4}'' \times \frac{3}{4}'' \times \frac{1}{8}''$ angle aluminum
2. $\frac{3}{4}''$ plywood
3. Screws

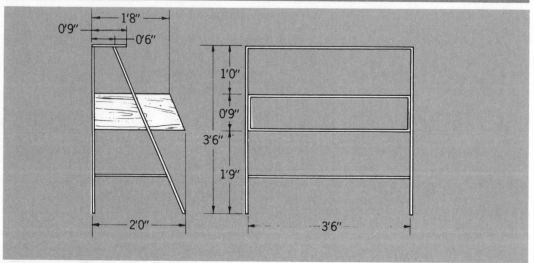

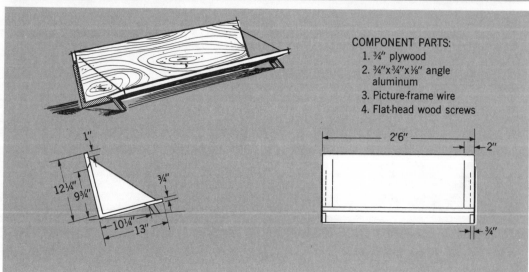

COMPONENT PARTS:
1. $\frac{3}{4}''$ plywood
2. $\frac{3}{4}'' \times \frac{3}{4}'' \times \frac{1}{8}''$ angle aluminum
3. Picture-frame wire
4. Flat-head wood screws

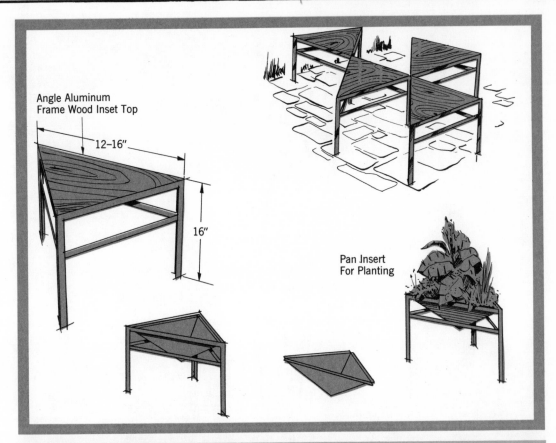

Angle Aluminum
Frame Wood Inset Top

12–16"

16"

Pan Insert
For Planting

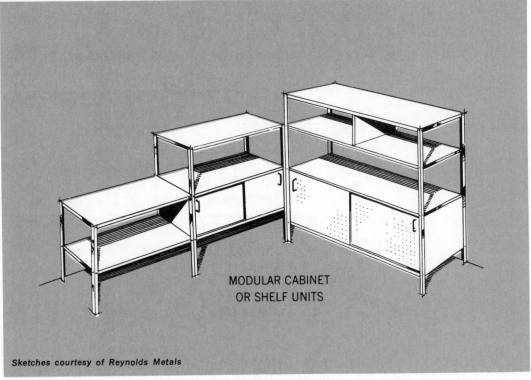

MODULAR CABINET
OR SHELF UNITS

Sketches courtesy of Reynolds Metals

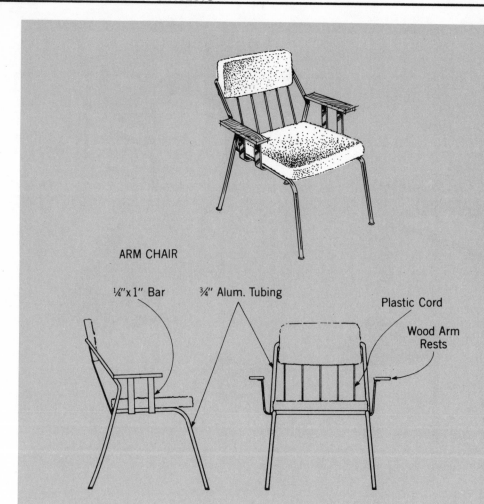

ARM CHAIR

¼"x 1" Bar   ¾" Alum. Tubing   Plastic Cord

Wood Arm
Rests

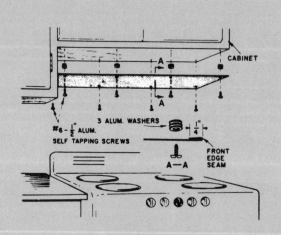

CABINET

A

A

3 ALUM. WASHERS   ¼"

#6 – ½" ALUM.
SELF TAPPING SCREWS

FRONT
EDGE
SEAM

A—A

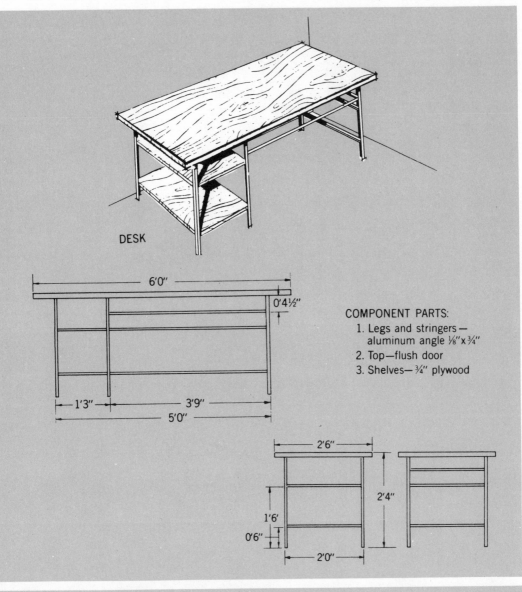

DESK

6'0"

0'4½"

1'3"   3'9"

5'0"

COMPONENT PARTS:
1. Legs and stringers—
   aluminum angle ⅛"x¾"
2. Top—flush door
3. Shelves—¾" plywood

2'6"

2'4"

1'6'

0'6"

2'0"

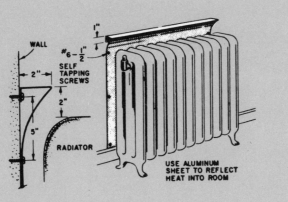

WALL

1"

#6 - 1½
SELF
TAPPING
SCREWS

2"

2"

5"

RADIATOR

USE ALUMINUM
SHEET TO REFLECT
HEAT INTO ROOM

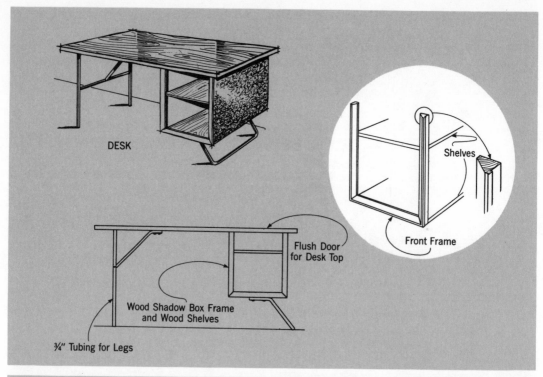

DESK

Flush Door
for Desk Top

Wood Shadow Box Frame
and Wood Shelves

¾" Tubing for Legs

Shelves

Front Frame

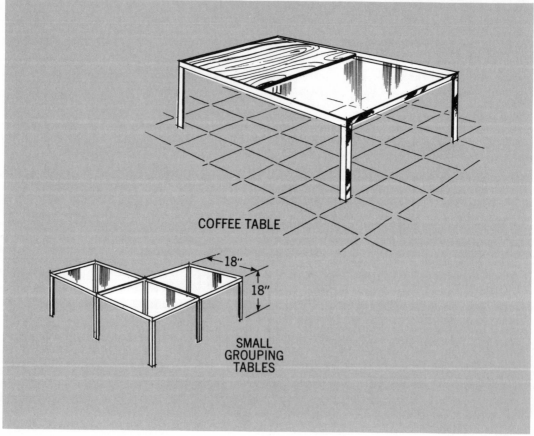

COFFEE TABLE

18"

18"

SMALL
GROUPING
TABLES

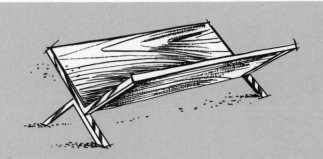

COMPONENT PARTS:
1. $^3_4''$ plywood
2. $^3_4'' \times {}^3_4'' \times {}^1_8''$ angle aluminum
3. Flat-head screws

RECORD OR BOOK SHELF

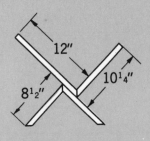

12"

$8^1_2''$ $10^1_4''$

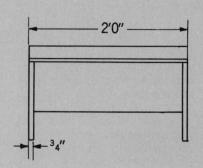

2'0"

$^3_4''$

ROOM DIVIDER

COMPONENT PARTS:
1. $^3_4'' \times {}^3_4'' \times {}^1_8''$ angle aluminum
2. $^3_4''$ plywood
3. Piano hinge for large door
4. Flat-head screws

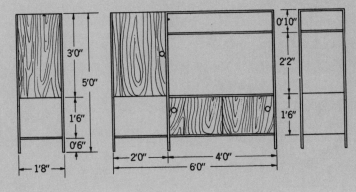

3'0"

5'0"

1'6"

0'6"

1'8"

0'10"

2'2"

1'6"

2'0"   4'0"

6'0"

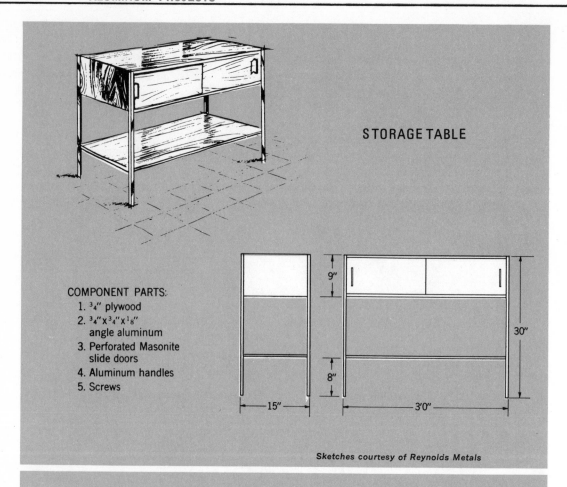

STORAGE TABLE

COMPONENT PARTS:
1. ³₄" plywood
2. ³₄" x ³₄" x ¹₈"
   angle aluminum
3. Perforated Masonite
   slide doors
4. Aluminum handles
5. Screws

9"

30"

8"

15"

3'0"

Sketches courtesy of Reynolds Metals

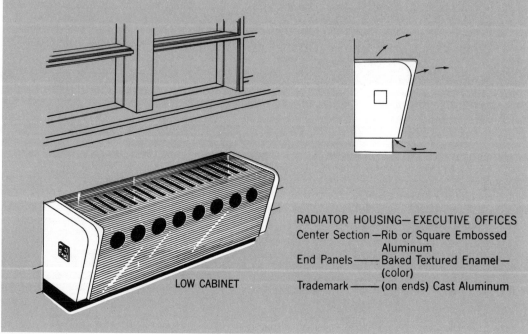

LOW CABINET

RADIATOR HOUSING— EXECUTIVE OFFICES
Center Section —Rib or Square Embossed
                    Aluminum
End Panels——Baked Textured Enamel—
                    (color)
Trademark——(on ends) Cast Aluminum

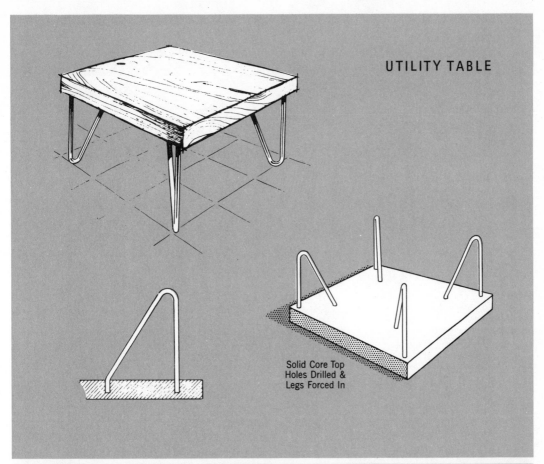

UTILITY TABLE

Solid Core Top
Holes Drilled &
Legs Forced In

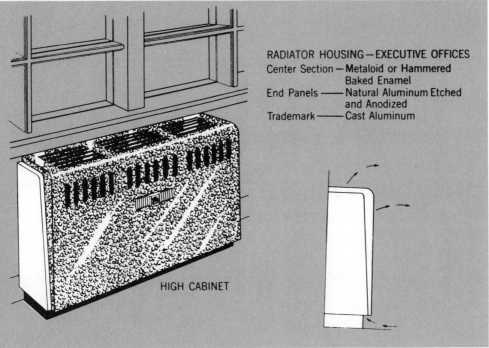

RADIATOR HOUSING—EXECUTIVE OFFICES
Center Section—Metaloid or Hammered
Baked Enamel
End Panels——Natural Aluminum Etched
and Anodized
Trademark——Cast Aluminum

HIGH CABINET

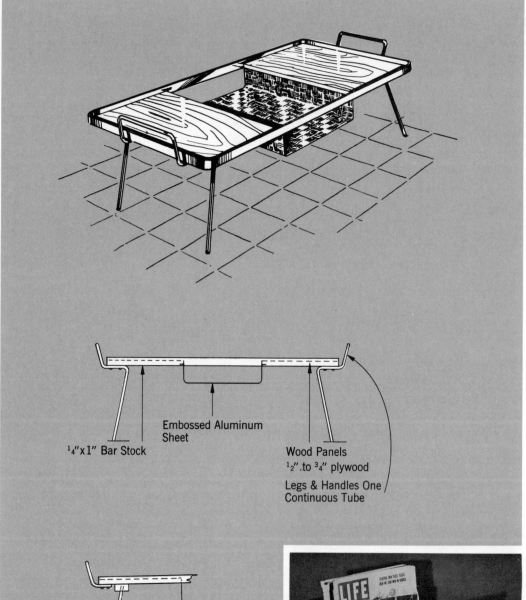

Embossed Aluminum
Sheet

$^1_4$"x1" Bar Stock

Wood Panels
$^1_2$".to $^3_4$" plywood

Legs & Handles One
Continuous Tube

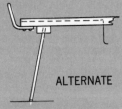

ALTERNATE

American Bond

This masonry term is used to describe a pattern of brick laying. It is the same as common bond. The American bond pattern is widely used for the bricks can be laid quickly and easily, even by the home handyman.

In this brick pattern, every fifth or sixth course or row of bricks consists of headers (bricks laid with the ends forward) while the other courses consists of stretchers (bricks laid with side edge forward)

Also see *BRICKS*.

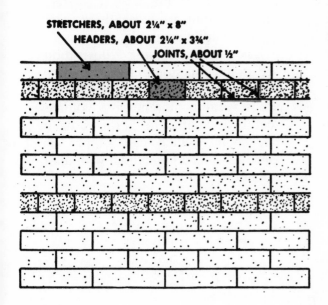

STRETCHERS, ABOUT 2¼" x 8"

HEADERS, ABOUT 2¼" x 3¾"

JOINTS, ABOUT ½"

Amplifier

An electronic device used in reproduction of sound for phonographs, radio and TV. The instrument magnifies or multiplies electrical impulses so that they are strong or powerful enough to actuate a loudspeaker.

Also see *HI-FI*.

Anatomy for Building

As a basic guide for the handymen interested in making their own kitchen cabinets, designing and building their own furniture or constructing built-ins for their home, here are the important standard measurements. While it is possible to rely upon your eye for judging graceful lines or proper proportions, there are certain dimensions in building for the home that are universal. They are followed by all architects, industrial designers and furniture designers. The seat of a chair, for example, must be 15″ to 18″ above the floor and the back must slope at an angle of 105° to the seat, if the chair is to be comfortable to sit in. That is comfortable for adults; for an average child of 11, the seat should be 14″ above the floor level.

Naturally, you take the dimensions of the chairs in your home for granted just as you do the height of the kitchen cabinets above the sink or the range. Yet, certain basic di-

mensions have been used by the people who planned them. In today's home, with the handyman doing more and more building, it is necessary for him to have these basic figures readily available.

The accompanying illustrations are an introduction to the art of planning, the anatomy of building. There are several comprehensive volumes readily available in libraries or in bookshops, which can supply the more advanced handyman with additional dimensions.

Comfort, when sitting in a chair, eating at a table or writing at a desk, is determined in part by the height of the chair or table. The height of basic furniture, such as chairs and tables, varies with age as noted.

	Table Height	Chair Height
	— in inches —	
Adults	29	18
14 to 18 years	26	16
8 to 14 years	24	14
4 to 8 years	22	12

MAXIMUM HEIGHTS

Maximum height is a determining factor not only when making furniture but also when constructing built-ins about the home. How high should it be? The heights specified in the accompanying illustration are normal for the average adult.

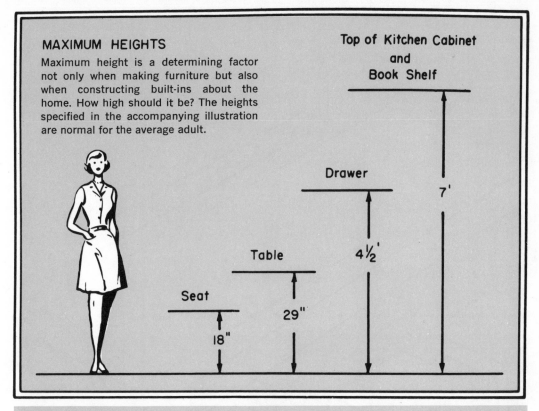

Elbow room is an important factor when planning a family dining table. There must be sufficient space not only for the place setting but for serving trays and dishes as well. Extra space never goes to waste.

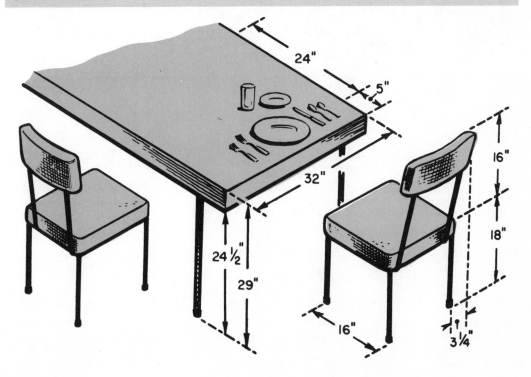

FOR THE SNACK COUNTER

Pass Thru To Dining Room

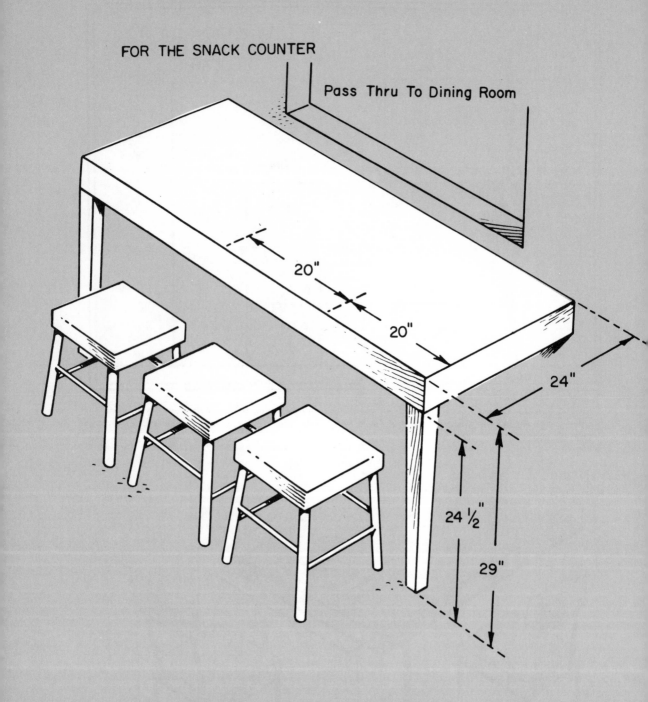

20"

20"

24"

24 ½"

29"

A breakfast bar is designed for a quick snack where elaborate table settings are never used. You can economize on space, allowing only 20″ for each person—man, woman or child.

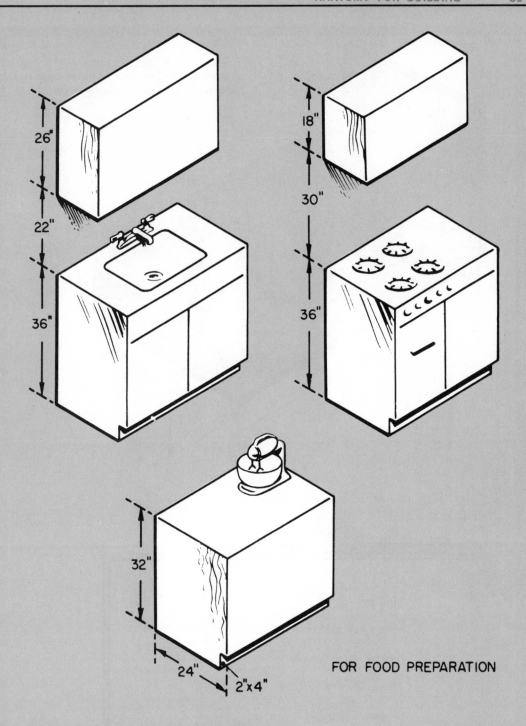

26"

22"

36"

18"

30"

36"

32"

24"

2"x4"

FOR FOOD PREPARATION

Efficient kitchen operation depends to a great extent upon the height of base cabinets. Toe space, along the lower front, is needed so that the housekeeper can work close to the cabinets. The most efficient height of counters used for food preparation is 32" above the floor. Near the sink and range, however, base cabinets should be about 36" from floor level, so that the tops of the cabinets are aligned with the appliances.

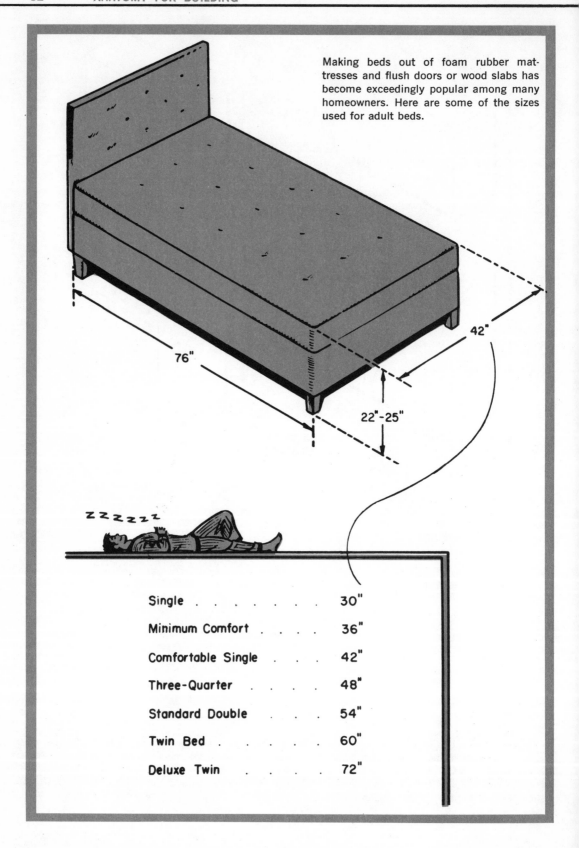

Making beds out of foam rubber mattresses and flush doors or wood slabs has become exceedingly popular among many homeowners. Here are some of the sizes used for adult beds.

76"

42"

22"-25"

zzzzzz

Single	30"
Minimum Comfort	36"
Comfortable Single	42"
Three-Quarter	48"
Standard Double	54"
Twin Bed	60"
Deluxe Twin	72"

FOR HANGING CLOTHES

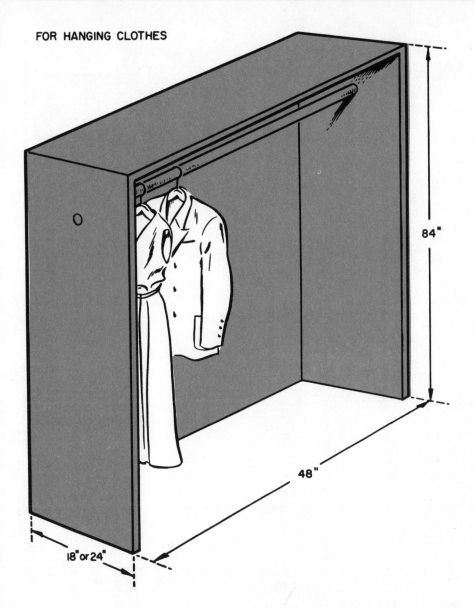

84"

48"

18" or 24"

Should you have insufficient closet space in your home, here's a handy guide to making that extra closet. It should be 84" high and about 48" wide—enough for a single adult. The depth of the closet is determined by the type of clothes pole used. If the pole is hung across the 48" closet width, then the closet should be at least 24" deep. If the pull-out type of clothes pole is used, only 18" depth is required.

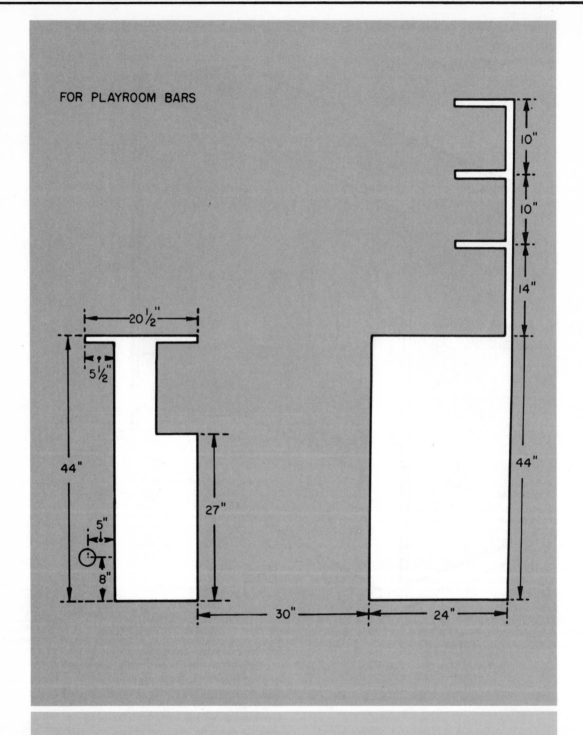

FOR PLAYROOM BARS

A bar in the recreation room or basement play area is a welcome addition to many homes. Here are the basic dimensions for the bar itself and the accompanying storage compartment and shelves behind it. For those who like a touch of realism and want to add a brass rail, note that it should be 8″ above the floor and 5″ out from the front face of the bar. Leave adequate aisle space between the bar and the storage wall behind it.

Anatomy for the Workshop

The right height for your workbench and your power tools is, to a great extent, determined by your height and your working habits. It is essential that the workbench be at a convenient height, one that will minimize fatigue, make the work easy to get at and be at the right level for various hand tool operations.

When mounting power tools on a stand, the correct height is important not only from a craftsman's viewpoint but also for safety's sake. In table form are some average heights for a workbench plus power tool stands. Remember, these are only averages; adjust them to meet your own needs.

Heights for the Workshop

Workbench	36"-40"
Table Saw	36"-38"
Shaper	36"
Jointer	32"-34"
Drill Press	48"
Band Saw	38"-40"
Jig Saw	38"-40"
Belt-Disc Sander	32"-34"
Lathe	38"-40"
Grinder	34"-36"

Anchors for Concrete

There are several ways for the handyman to attach wood or metal to masonry, either concrete or brick.

Anchors extruded of Tenite plastic secure nails or screws in practically any solid material, such as brick, plaster or cinder blocks. The anchor is hammered into a pre-drilled hole and then the screw or nail is inserted. The anchors come in all screw sizes and provide safe anchoring for anything from pantry shelves to heavy-duty electrical conduit.

Photo courtesy Tennessee Eastman Co.

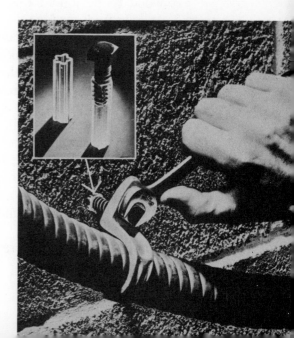

He encounters this type of an anchoring problem when he:

- installs studding or furring strips prior to erecting walls for a finished basement.
- adds metal shelf brackets inside a concrete block garage.
- secures electrical conduit to the outside of a brick house. The most commonly used method of anchoring to concrete or brick is the lag bolt and anchor unit. The anchor, which resembles a tube, can be made of lead, fiber or plastic. It is necessary to drill a hole in the masonry with a star drill and hammer or a masonry bit and electric drill; the hole should be the same diameter as the anchor. Insert the anchor in the hole and set the lag bolt through the piece to be fastened to the masonry into the anchor.

However, if you wish to avoid the drilling of holes for anchors, you can use:

- *steel cut nails,* commonly called flooring nails. Merely hammer the nail through the piece of wood to be joined to the concrete or brick surface.
- *concrete nails,* which have oversized heads and shanks. It is necessary to pre-drill the wood in order to avoid splitting. Drill a hole that is slightly over-sized for the shank of the nail, set the nail in place and hammer it into the masonry. This type of concrete anchor is used primarily to hold pipe clips, which are used to secure electrical conduit to masonry.
- *adhesive nails,* which resemble

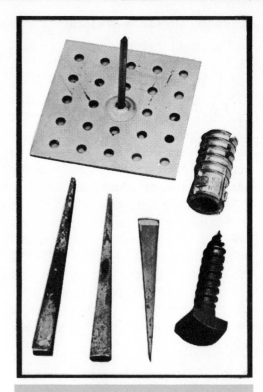

There are many types of anchors which can be used in concrete, cinder block, bricks and stone. Here are a few of the anchors any home handyman can use easily.

over-sized thumb tacks with perforated square heads. A blob of adhesive spread over the head secures it to the concrete or brick, no matter how rough the surface is. The board is then driven into the nail, which projects out from the wall. After the board is in place, the sharp tip of the nail is hammered over and back into the wood.

Anchors for Walls

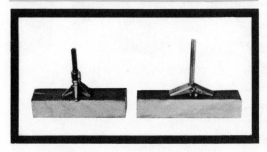

Spring and solid head toggle bolts are used for anchoring to walls where the surface is too thin to retain a screw or nail.

What they look like from the other side— on left is a Molly fastener. Note how spider legs draw up toward the head to hold this anchor in place. Spring toggle (right) is also an efficient wall anchor. Note hole through piece of wood (or wall when you are using it) must be large enough for the spring head to pass through in a folded position.

While a picture hook, nail or screw is usually sufficient to secure a picture or mirror to a wall, there are times when the weight of the object to be hung is too great to use these anchoring devices safely. Unless the nail or screw goes through the wall into wood (either a stud or lath), it will be unable to do the job.

The technique of securing a wall anchor depends, in part, upon the type of material used for the wall. For a plaster wall, you can drill a hole, insert a Rawl plug and then set a screw into it. This is similar to the lag bolt and anchor method used in masonry.

However, with the greater use of dry wall construction in homes today—plasterboard, Sheetrock, plywood—another more positive form of wall anchor is needed. These are Mollies, a special anchoring device which expands inside the wall. Mollies are made for use in plaster or dry walls. Here, in step by step form, is the technique for attaching any anchor of this type:

- Drill a hole in the wall of the same diameter as the Molly.
- Remove the screw from the anchor and hammer the body of the anchor into the wall. Make certain that the teeth under the anchor head are imbedded in the wall material.
- Replace the screw and tighten as far as possible. This action

compresses the anchor within the wall.

- After the anchor is secured, remove the screw and set it through the bracket or wood to be attached to the wall; then place the end of the screw into the hole in the anchor. Tighten the screw until the work is secured to the wall.

Toggle bolts can also be used when a material or object must be secured to plaster, gypsum wallboard or other surface of thin material that will not directly retain a screw or nail. There are two types of toggle bolts, spring head and solid head. The holding power varies with the type of bolt and increases with size. The screw section of the bolt cannot be removed without loss of the anchor, as can be done with the Molly fastener.

Angle Bead

This is a special molding similar in shape to an angle iron but instead made of wood or other material. It is used where two walls meet at right angles to conceal the joint formed by the two walls.

There are many different angle bead moldings available as stock moldings in lumber yards.

Angle Divider

The angle divider serves a multitude of purposes. It functions in a manner somewhat the same as a T-bevel in marking off identical angles

Basic parts of an angle divider.

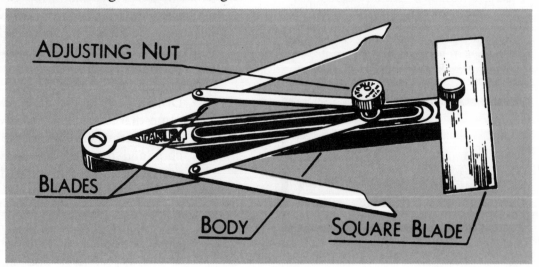

on several pieces of work. It is also used to find the center of two pieces of wood joined at an angle.

Laying off a miter with an angle divider. The square blade may be used for a try square when working on a surface.

Sketches from "Tool Guide" courtesy of Stanley Tools

The angle divider is a double bevel. It is used to take off and divide angles for the miter cut in one operation. The handle is graduated on the back for laying off 5, 6, 8 and 10 sided work.

Angle Iron

Basically, this is a shaped piece of metal, in which the sides form a 90° angle. It has many household uses, such as lintels above window and door openings in brick and brick veneer homes. It is also used in metal furniture, for a length of angle iron is stronger than equivalent bar or flat stock.

This term is also used to describe one type of metal fastener which is used to reinforce and repair wood joints. Usually made of steel, they are available in different sizes and thicknesses. They come with pre-drilled holes to take flathead screws. In this way, the head of the screw is flush with the metal surface when the angle iron is attached. Angle irons can also be used to join metal to metal or wood. In these cases, sheet metal screws or flathead bolts and nuts may be used as the fastening device.

Angle irons are used to reinforce or repair wood joints when the two pieces of wood are joined at a right angle or 90°.

Angle Valve

Basically a globe valve in design and operation, it acts both as a valve and an elbow. The inlet and outlet pipes are at right angles to each other.

Angle valves have many uses within the home. Large size units are used to connect the steam riser coming upright through the floor to the radiator. Smaller models, frequently brass- or chrome-plated, are used to connect the water supply line coming out of the bathroom wall to the flush tank with the water closet.

Also see *VALVES*.

An angle valve.

Antenna Outlet

There are special outlets or receptacles, as they are technically called, and plugs made to connect TV antenna wires or radio aerial and ground wires to the set. The receptacle and plug are designed so that they cannot be inadvertently connected into the household electrical system. One "leg" of the plug and a "slot" of the outlet are set at an angle and do not match standard electrical fixtures—a worthwhile safety precaution.

The receptacle is of the Despard variety which requires a special plate for mounting inside the ordinary out-

The receptacle has the antenna and ground connections clearly printed on the face of the unit. Note the angled position of the "slot" in the receptacle and the "leg" of the plug. This is a safeguard to prevent connecting the radio or TV into the house's electrical circuit.

let box set in the walls of a home. There are, however, Despard electrical fixtures made so that the ground-aerial receptacle can be set into the same outlet box as a receptacle connected to the house's power lines. Both the aerial and ground connections are clearly printed on the face of the receptacle and the plug can be wired to match.

While designed primarily for aerial and ground connections, this type of receptacle and plug is often used by Hi-Fi enthusiasts who wish to install extra speaker outlets in different parts of their home. The speaker output wires from the amplifier are connected to the receptacle and the plug is connected to the lead wires from the speaker. The use of brass and silver colored "legs" on the plugs makes it possible to wire the speakers in proper phase with each other.

Also see *DESPARD FIXTURES, ELECTRICAL WIRING* and *HI-FI.*

Antiquing

You can alter the finish of your furniture so that instead of its having an "old" look it takes on the appearance of a charming "antique." The first step is to remove the finish which now covers the wood. Use commercial paint remover which you can get at the paint store, then rub with sandpaper until a smooth surface is obtained. Start with coarse sandpaper, and finish with 00.

Paint the surface with enamel undercoater. If your furniture is carved, be careful that the grooves in the carving do not become filled with paint. After the surface is completely dry, paint a coat of light-colored enamel over it. Here, too, you must watch out for the carving, to avoid filling the grooves. The color you choose for this enamel coat depends on your decorating theme; you may use the lightest tones of either buff, gray, green, blue, or pink, or even white.

Your next step is the glazing. In a shallow dish, mix together 1½ teaspoonfuls of burnt turkey umber, 3 tablespoonfuls of turpentine, and 1 tablespoonful of clear varnish. With a small, soft brush, apply this glaze to the wood surface. Work slowly, and don't cover more than about a 3 sq. foot area at a time, as the glaze dries rapidly. Keep some clean rags at hand, and after you glaze an area wipe over it with delicate strokes; this will produce a grained effect. If the results do not please you, quickly wipe off the glaze with a rag dipped in turpentine. Then go over the area again with the glaze, and wipe with a clean rag, until you get just the right effect. Apply this glaze-and-wipe process over the next area, until you have covered the entire surface and "antiqued" it to your satisfaction.

If the weather is damp or rainy, wait for the next clear day. Use clear varnish to give the wood its preserving process. Dip a clean brush heavily into the varnish, and let the varnish "flow" over the wood surface. Brush with long strokes, from one end of the surface to the other. Then brush in the opposite direction over the varnished surface, and brush over that in the first direction you had taken.

You will see a very glossy finish, when the varnish dries. Now is the time to rub it, using a soft cloth first dipped in a light oil (such as sewing machine oil), then dipped in finely powdered pumice. Rub the cloth gently over the surface, to roughen the varnish yet not to rub it off. This will produce a "satiny" finish. The final touch is to remove the dust gently from the surface with a dry, clean cloth, exerting no pressure.

Also see *FURNITURE FINISHES*.

Anvil

A steel or iron block for forging or hammering. Now some vises come with an anvil block as part of the vise. The handyman will find an anvil helpful when rivetting or when doing metal work.

This is a molding or casing generally used under a window sill inside the home. Its purpose is to conceal any opening between the sill and rough sill, which is set between the interior and exterior walls of the house. The apron is nailed in place so that it is flush with the sill stool and the interior wall.

In some homes with masonry exteriors—brick, concrete block, brick veneer—the outside sill is made of concrete or brick instead of wood. In fact, in some homes with casement windows, the sill is level—the top surface of the concrete or brick. However, no matter what the exterior design pattern is, an apron is used within the home.

The apron not only hides any unsightly opening in the window framing but it also helps to keep drafts from entering the home or heat from

Apron

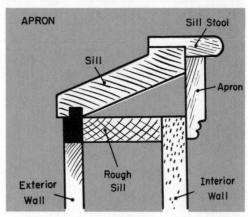

escaping too rapidly through the walls in the winter.

A small semicircular molding can be used to cover the joint between two sections of wall material, such as plywood, hardboard or any other type of dry wall material. These moldings can be plain or ornamental.

Aquastat

An aquastat is an integral part of a hot water heating system. It is a thermal-controlled switch which regulates temperature of water in the

hot water heating system.

Also see *HEATING SYSTEMS.*

Arbor and Trellis

The terms "arbor" and "trellis" are generally used interchangeably; however, the former is the heavier archway structure under which people walk, whereas the trellis need be only a latticework of wood strips as a support for climbing plants.

Arbor

This must be strong enough to

carry the weight of flowers and foliage which you train over the framework. The structure can be made simply by securely setting rows of tall wood posts into the ground, and nailing boards across them at the top. They may be straight across, or come to a point in the center or, if you want a rounded arch, use lightweight upright wood strips and bend them to

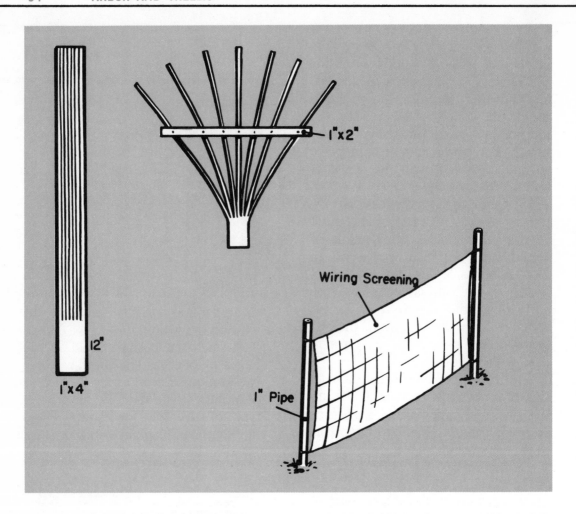

form the arch. To secure them in place, nail horizontal strips across them at regularly-spaced intervals.

The upright sides of the arbor are also strengthened by nailing across horizontal strips, forming a crisscross, straight or diagonal pattern.

Use rustproof nails and outdoor paint to withstand the weather.

Trellis

This is usually built against a fence or the wall of the house or garage, and vines and other climbing plants are trained over the trellis. It is often constructed to stand on its own, without being supported by a wall.

The design of the trellis depends on your own taste, the space in your garden or backyard, the materials you use. Wood is most generally used. Upright strips are secured in the ground, and horizontal strips are nailed across, in crisscross, straight or diagonal pattern.

If the trellis is against the house or garage, paint the wood to match the color of the structure against which it rests; this gives an uncluttered appearance to the house exterior. Here, too, use outdoor paint and rustproof nails.

A trellis is sometimes made of rope or wire, stretched and nailed in a pattern against a fence or wall. This is not recommended for heavy vines, but it serves the purpose for lighter-weight plants. The rope or wire should be sturdy enough to withstand weather conditions.

6 Simple Trellises and Arbors

1. This fan-shaped trellis can be made in less than an hour. If you have a power saw, the whole job will take only a few minutes. All you need is a 6′ length of 1x4 and a 30″ piece of 1x2. It is best if you make the trellis out of redwood, which is weather-resistant and decay-proof. Just mark off ½″ intervals along the edge of the 1x4 and make parallel saw cuts as shown, leaving the bottom 12″ uncut. Then take the piece of 1x2 and nail the extended ½″ strips to it with two 3d aluminum nails into each strip. You can use rustproof screws if you wish in place of the nails.

2. Another very simple trellis can be made by sinking two 1″ diameter pipes into the earth. Sink about 18″ to 24″ and leave anywhere from 60″ to 72″ exposed above the ground level. Buy rustproof screening and attach it to each of the posts. You can wind a thin wire through the openings in the screening just as would be done when sewing. This makes an attractive trellis but can be used only for light-weight climbers. Do not use heavy vines unless you use "hardware cloth"—a heavy screening—between the two pipes. Most hardware stores sell hardware cloth screening with ½″ spaces.

3. A rectangular trellis with woven vertical and horizontal pieces can be built out of 1x2 lumber and ½x1

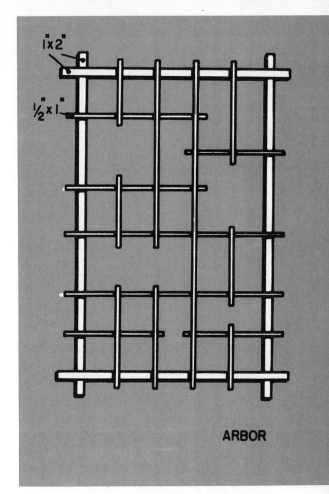

ARBOR

strips, both of which are readily available at any lumber yard. The two outside pieces and the top and bottom cross pieces of this trellis are made out of 1x2's held with two rust-proof screws at each joint. The other sections of the trellis are cut out of ½x1 strips and nailed in place with 2 aluminum nails at each joint. These strips can run the full length vertically and horizontally or can be attached in an open weave form as shown in this sketch.

4. If you have heavy vines or wish to have your trellis stand free, away from any additional support, such as a house or garage, make it out of

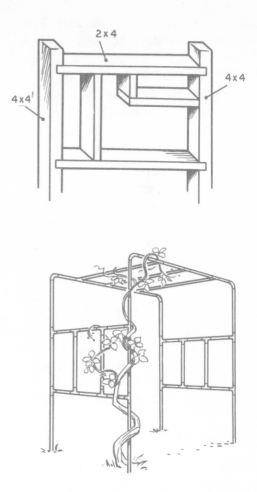

heavier lumber. This free-form model is made out of 2x4's and 4x4's, preferably redwood. However, you can use cedar or cypress if either of these is more readily available. The two upright posts plus the top and base horizontal supports are made of 4x4's. The corners are jointed by cutting dado joints, or toe-nail the pieces in place. Cut pieces of 2x4 redwood for the inner members of this trellis and toe-nail in place with aluminum nails.

5. An easy-to-make arbor is built along the same lines as the heavy vine trellis. The uprights at each end are cut out of 4x4 redwood, cedar or cypress. If you use pine, coat the lumber with a wood preservative and paint with a quality outdoor paint. The top cross sections at each end are also cut out of 4x4 stock. The arbor should be at least 6' 6" high and a minimum of 40" wide. How far apart you set the two end posts depends upon the size you wish to make your arbor. If this distance is 5' or less, you can nail lattice strips across the top. If the space is 5' to 7' use 1x2 lumber.

6. Maybe you'd like to make your arbor out of craftworker's aluminum. There are special fittings available in retail stores selling this aluminum which enable you to join the tubing stock. Use either 1" or 1¼" diameter tubing for the arbor. The corner joints are secured by using 90° elbows. The other joining of the tubing is done with T-butt connectors. You have an almost unlimited choice of designs from which to select. Plan your arbor by drawing it to scale on paper; then purchase the necessary parts and you will find that the entire job will take only a few hours to complete.

Architectural Symbols

If you like to make your own plans in fixing up your house, or if you want to know how to read blueprints, these symbols are used universally in the building trades.

Also see *HOUSE PLANS*.

BUILDING CONSTRUCTION

Tile	Cast concrete block
Earth	Insulation: Loose fill
Plaster	Board or quilts
Sheet metal	Cut stone
Built-in cabinet	Ashlar
Outside door: Brick wall	Shingles (siding)
Frame wall	Wood, rough
Inside door: Frame wall	Wood, finished
Brick	Cased or arched openings
Firebrick	Single casement window
Concrete	Double-hung windows

Double casement window

ARCHITECTURAL ABBREVIATIONS

BRK	Brick	GI	Galvanized
CI	Cast iron	GL	Glass
CLG	Ceiling	INT	Interior
CEM	Cement	K	Kitchen
CONC	Concrete	LR	Living room
DR	Dining room	MC	Medicine chest
DHW	Double hung window	OC	On center
EXT	Exterior	PLAS	Plaster
FIN	Finish	TC	Terra cotta
FL	Floor	WI	Wrought iron

PLUMBING

Bath tubs:		Toilets:	
Corner		Tank	
Free standing		Flush valve	
Floor drain		Urinals:	
		Stall-type	
Shower drain		Wall-hung	
Hot-water tank	H.W.T.	Laundry trays	
Grease trap		Built-in shower	
Hose bibb or sill cock		Shower	
Lavatories:		Sinks:	
Pedestal		Single drain board.	
Wall-hung		Double drain board.	
Corner			

ELECTRICAL

Pull switch	P.S.	Ceiling outlet	
Single-pole switch	S₁	Wall bracket	
Double-pole switch	S₂	Single convenience outlet	
Triple-pole switch	S₃	Double convenience outlet	
Buzzer		Ceiling outlet, gas & electric	
Floor outlet		Motor	
Bell		Light outlet with wiring and switches indicated	
Drop cord			

HEATING, VENTILATING AND APPLIANCE

HEATING, VENTILATING AND APPLIANCE

Supply duct _____	⊠ (S)
Exhaust duct _____	⊠ (E)
Heat register _____	R
Radiator, recessed _____	「RAD」
Radiator _____	RAD
Water heater _____	(WH)
Automatic washer _____	AW
Dishwasher _____	DW
Telephone _____	◄

Archway

The large, open archway between two rooms, or leading from the hall, may be closed up if you desire. A pair of French doors could be hung inside the archway. Or, if you wish more wall space and a single door, the archway could have built-in shelves on either side, for books and ornaments, and the door hung in the center between the two rows of shelves.

If you don't want to close the archway permanently, but desire a temporary closing, a wide folding screen or a pair of screens will fulfill that function adequately. The screens could be covered decoratively, or painted a solid color to match the wall.

Also see *ACCORDION-FOLD DOORS, BUILT-INS* and *ROOM DIVIDERS*.

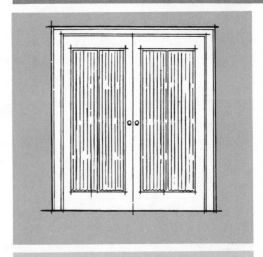

1. A pair of French doors can be set within a framework set into an arch between two rooms. If you wish, you can make your own door frames, using corrugated Fiberglas as the interior material within the door frame. For framing around the doors, see **Door Framing**.

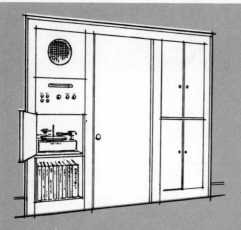

2. If there's a wide opening between the two rooms, you can put the space to use with a built-in. Here on the left wall is a Hi-Fi unit—tuner, phonograph and record storage, plus the speaker. Sliding cabinets provide storage of other items to the right of the door.

3. If you still want an open feeling but prefer a definite separation between the two rooms, follow this technique. Two base frames about 36″ to 48″ are made of plywood with trim molding added on the outside. Large columns are used to tie the base in with the ceiling.

4. Round archways present more of a problem but here too the problem is easily solved. Toe-nail a double 2 x 4 across the top of the opening to make a square frame for folding doors. Use panels of opaque glass set in wood trim molding to fill in the top.

5. Decorative screens, finished in a wallpaper to match that on the walls, can be used to seal one room off from the other. If you want that open feeling at times, just move the screens aside. Screens are easily made out of 2 x 2 lumber and plywood.

This material has many uses. It comes in dry form, packed in bags of 100 lbs. or less, and is mixed with water for purposes of insulating heating system pipes. Asbestos cement is also made into wallboard and shin-

Asbestos Cement

gles for use on the exterior of the house.

The separate uses of asbestos cement are included in their specific sections throughout these volumes.

This is a versatile material of many uses. It is a binding element in cement mixtures, and is used in paving driveways and to waterproof basements. Asphalt is also processed into floor tiles, and roof shingles.

Asphalt

The various uses of asphalt are included in their separate sections throughout these volumes.

This economical composition flooring material can be laid over concrete directly on the ground. It is made of asphalt, asbestos or mineral fibers and pigments.

Asphalt tiles generally come in squares 9"x 9" but other sizes and shapes are available, varying depending upon the manufacturer. They come in a full range of hues but colors are neutralized.

These tiles are easy to maintain— mopping with soap or detergent and water and then waxing. They are the least expensive of the composition floorings. While they will stand tough wear, asphalt tiles can be cracked by

Asphalt Tile

impact or dented by the weight of heavy furniture.

Also see *FLOOR TILES*.

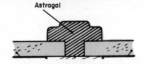

A small semicircular molding can be used to cover the joint between two sections of wall material, such as

Astragal

plywood, hardboard or any other type of dry wall material. These moldings can be either plain or ornamental.

Attics

A complete one room apartment in what was formerly an unused attic space. The entire installation was a do-it-yourself project including most of the furniture.

Photograph courtesy of Armstrong Cork Co.

Converting an attic to greater usefulness is a project that anyone can undertake without too much trouble using the basic handyman tools. The starting point in the conversion project is to clean out the attic. Sift through the things which you have accumulated there. Probably many of these items can be used and put to work in the project. The next step, and the hardest, is to throw out the items that cannot be used. Remember that in your construction you will be able to make room for limited storage space under the eaves. After you have put in the partitions to convert the majority of the floor area into rooms you will need, you can plan the under-eaves storage space for a variety of items in drawers and on shelves.

A typical attic conversion will require the various tools and materials which are listed. You won't need all of this material immediately if you plan to finish your attic in easy stages and do a room at a time. This list is your starting point but the exact amount of equipment and material you use will be determined by the size of your project and the amount of work you plan to do yourself.

Install a subfloor so that you can work and move around without crashing through the ceiling of the room below. This installation is of tongue-and-groove flooring. Plywood sheets can also be used.

Photograph courtesy Owens-Corning Fiberglas Corp.

Hints and Suggestions on Attic Planning and Construction

1. Check with your lumber yard and building supply dealer for his advice and valuable tips. Show him your rough sketch. He can suggest material which is practical, easy to handle and inexpensive.

2. Plan your attic bathroom or plumbing installation so that it is above the other bathroom in the main portion of the house to simplify installation work and reduce the amount of pipe necessary for the conversion project.

3. Check into the various finance plans wth easy payments offered by some lumber yards for home repairs and remodeling.

4. To cut costs, make your own doors of 1x4 lumber frames which are then sandwiched between hardboard, plywood or other decorative material. For a decorative touch, use brass headed upholstery nails to form various patterns and designs.

5. During the pencil and paper stage of your attic planning try to include as many built-in features as possible. These can be used for storage, furniture, work surfaces and seating arrangements. You will find that designing and building these features will save you money on furnishings for the new space.

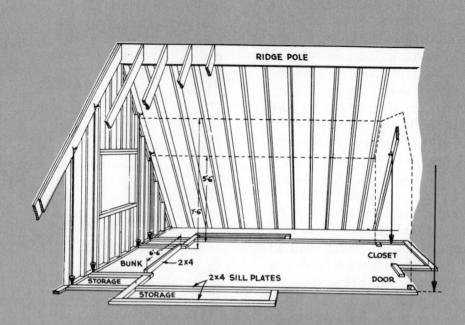

RIDGE POLE

BUNK   2x4

STORAGE

2x4 SILL PLATES

STORAGE

CLOSET

DOOR

TYPICAL FRAMING FOR ATTIC ROOM

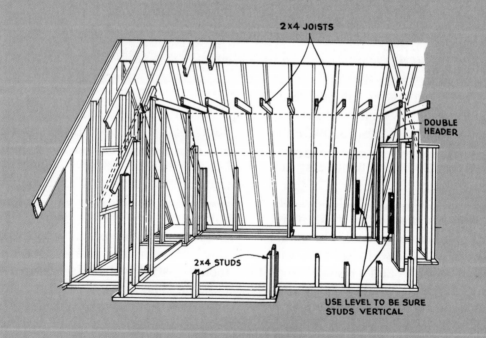

2x4 JOISTS

DOUBLE HEADER

2x4 STUDS

USE LEVEL TO BE SURE STUDS VERTICAL

Sketches courtesy of Skil Corp.

6. Collect the pamphlets brochures and material supplied by the manufacturers to lumber yards and magazines to help you in your planning construction.

7. Prevent possible cold drafts by packing insulation around window frames and sills.

8. To lay out angular cuts for boards and any of the wall material which are to fit under eaves, measure the height from the floor at two points the width of the piece apart, mark them on the board or wall material and draw a straight line between these two points.

9. Secure the services of a qualified heating contractor to install the extensions from your existing heating plant.

10. Sound-deadening felt may be placed between the finished flooring and the subfloor for good inexpensive noise control.

Glossary of Attic Construction Terms

FRAMING—2 x 4's, 2 x 3's, etc., are dimensions of lumber for supporting the material which is used to form partitions and walls.

FURRING—Strips of wood, usually 1 x 2 or 1 x 3, applied to wall, ceiling or other surface to even it. Furring strips also provide an air space and form a base for the application of various types of wall coverings.

HEADER—A horizontal member between the studs over window and door openings. Usually the same dimensions as the stud lumber.

JAMB—This term includes the sides of door and window openings.

JOIST—A horizontal supporting member to which the floor and ceiling are fastened.

KNEE-WALL—A low partition for the wall formed by the studs running from the sloping ceiling rafters to the floor or base plates.

PARTITION—A dividing wall within any story of the building.

PLATE—This term defines the horizontal member placed at the top (top plate) and at the bottom (sole plate) of studs. It is nailed into position to form the wall or partition.

PLUMB—Means that the material or lumber is in a perfectly vertical position.

RAFTER—The structural member, generally sloping, of a roof.

RIDGE—The highest horizontal member of a roof to which the upper ends of the rafters are fastened.

SHIM—The term used to refer to building up behind furring or other construction member. It provides a solid backing and a true flush surface. Shimming is usually done with a wedge shaped piece of wood.

2 x 4's are nailed down as floor plates and vertical studs are put in place to mark off the partitions and walls. The couple above are installing knee-walls, usually at least four feet tall.

Photograph courtesy Owens-Corning Fiberglas Corp.

Construction Materials Needed

1. 2x3 or 2x4 framing lumber
2. 1x2 furring strips (for plank-type finishes)
3. Fiberglas, wool, batt, or granule insulation
4. Nails (several sizes)
5. Wall finish (plywood, gypsum, composition board)
6. Floor covering (linoleum, tile, carpeting)
7. Wood trim (moldings of various kinds)
8. Sub-flooring lumber
9. Flooring lumber
10. Flooring underlayment and felt
11. Mastic (for floor tile)
12. Doors
13. Windows or dormers
14. Plaster and lath (optional)
15. Heating equipment
16. Electrical wiring, lighting, outlets, switches
17. Plumbing connections
18. Custom made built-ins
19. Wallpaper
20. Paint
21. Hardware and fixtures
22. Window glass, mirrors, etc.
23. Ceiling material, board or tiles

Photographs courtesy of Owens-Corning Fiberglas Corp.

Collar beams or ceiling joists are installed at a minimum height of 7½'. They may be cut from 2 x 4's and nailed to the existing ceiling joists.

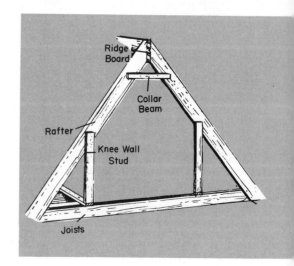

STUD—A vertical member in a wall or partition.

TOENAIL—To drive nails into a surface at an angle.

BASEBOARD—The wood trim at the bottom of the wall next to the floor.

BASE SHOE—A wood molding over the joint formed by the baseboard and the finished floor.

CLINCH—To drive nails through the lumber and bend the extended points back into the wood.

O.C.—On centers (from center to center i.e., 16″ on center).

Tools

The following are the basic tools necessary for framing and partitioning the attic: Hammer, saw, screw driver, carpenter's level, square, rule and some wooden horses or a short ladder.

How to Plan

It is always better to work with paper and pencil. If you can get a plan of your house from the builder use it as a guide. Measure floor space in the attic and make a scale drawing using 1″ to represent 1′. The division of the attic space depends upon your personal needs as well as the final use of the space. There is virtually an unlimited number of layouts you can plan for the attic conversion. Manufacturers of building materials and lumber dealers can supply you with pamphlets and brochures suggesting various layouts and designs for attic bedrooms, apartments, dens and living rooms. Custom made built-ins, also described and illustrated in the brochures, should be provided for and can be tailored to the space requirements. Study a number of these dealer suggestions to see which are suited to your physical needs, your financial abilities and your craftsmanship. Don't cut a board or hammer a nail until you have set down on paper a plan of operation and a general plan of the floor plan of the attic. When you have reached this point in your preparations it is a good idea to visit your lumber dealer with your plans and specifications. He can advise you about the types and advantages of the material you will need, give you building tips and can tell you what specific tools you will need.

Proceed in an organized fashion to finish your attic. In this way you will make the job easier, will keep a check on your progress and will avoid costly and time-consuming mistakes. The following steps are suggested as a guide and checklist:

1. Check the attic for electrical, heating and plumbing lines. If none have been provided, they are your major and first consideration.

2. If no subfloor has been installed or you have a walk down the center, lay the subfloor.

3. For more headroom and light, install a gable or shed dormer.

Partition studs are installed after the new wall and ceiling are placed. 2 x 4's are used and the partitions may be assembled on the floor then raised into place.

Make sure you provide for lighting, wiring, and plumbing. Check local building codes concerning these installations; it may be required to have such work done by licensed electricians or plumbers.

4. Nail knee-wall studs and ceiling joists, called collar beams.

5. Locate and erect partition walls to separate one room from another and make door frames.

6. Install the wiring for fixtures, switches and outlets, or have contractor do so if local building code requires it.

7. If you are adding a bathroom to the attic, have plumbing lines installed according to local code requirements.

8. Choose your insulation and install according to manufacturers' instructions.

9. Install the ceiling and wall materials.

10. Add selected finish floor over attic subfloor.

11. Install decorative trim to cover floor, wall and ceiling joints. Add trim around windows and doors.

12. Design built-ins and install them in the finished rooms.

13. Paint, wallpaper and finish ceiling, wall surfaces, built-ins and woodwork.

14. Install light fixtures, wall switches and wall outlets.

15. Move in furnishings and equipment.

Basic Framing for Attic Walls and Ceilings

The basic framing of an attic is comprised of the following steps:
1. Laying of the subfloor if the joists are exposed.
2. Join sloping roof with floor by erecting knee-walls.
3. Locate and install collar beams to form frame for ceiling.
4. Lay out and construct partition walls to divide attic into rooms.

Install the Subfloor

Installation of the subfloor will permit you to work and move about freely without danger of crashing through the ceiling of the room below. There are two types of subflooring you can install. One is tongue-and-groove flooring, which is rough sheathing lumber installed on the diagonal across the joists. The second is the ¾″ subfloor plywood. The plywood is much easier to install and saves a considerable amount of time. Nail the 4x8 plywood panels across the joists with 8-penny flooring nails, spaced 8″ apart.

Also see *SUBFLOOR*.

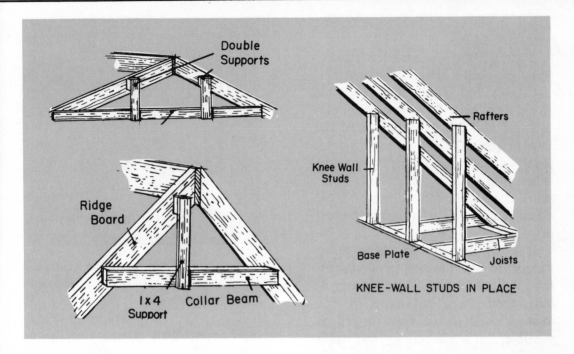

KNEE-WALL STUDS IN PLACE

Erecting the Knee-Walls

The minimum height advisable for knee-walls is at least 4'. Make sure that you provide for this height when you are locating the position for the floor plates. The knee-wall studs to form the attic side walls are attached to a base (floor) plate and the rafters. The base plate lumber should be the same dimension as the studs.

a. Line the base plate up to form lower edge of wall; nail through the subfloor into joists below with 16-penny nails.

b. Measure height of knee-wall stud from the base plate to the rafter above and cut studs to size, allowing one for each rafter.

c. Toe-nail stud to base plate with 8-penny nails and nail to side of rafters. Use a carpenter's level to make certain that studs are level.

To save time in checking level, erect first and last studs, check with level and stretch taut string between the two studs, using the string as guides to placement of other studs in the line.

When installing the knee-walls you may want to save some of the under-eaves space for storage; in this case do not attach studs in the storage areas. Frame this area by attaching a plate, the same size lumber as the studs, between the two studs forming the outside of the storage area.

Check the rafter spacing. Nearly all roof rafters are spaced on 16", 20" or 24" centers to take advantage of the standard widths of blanket insulation. This spacing determines the space between the knee-wall 2x4's. If your rafters are not regularly spaced you may have to erect "false" rafters or cut insulation blankets to fit.

Installing the Collar Beams

Many building codes specify that the bottom of the ceiling joist shall be a minimum of 7'6" from the floor. Since it is difficult to install a ceiling at an angle, collar beams or ceiling joists are added.

If the ceiling joists are less than 6′ long use 2x3's. For wider ceilings, use 2x4's and secure these joists to the rafters with 16-penny nails. Use a single nail to tack one end of the 2x4 in place at the correct height, level, and attach to the rafter at the other side with a single nail. Now, mark the length for cutting and use this piece as a pattern to cut the rest of your ceiling joists.

It is not necessary to add an extra support to hold the joist in narrow attics, if your ceiling joist is over 8′ long, then use a 1x4 nailed to the joist as close to the ridge board as possible. On a 12′ ceiling joist use a double support—one on each side of the ridge board.

You will need ventilation over your insulation for vapor control and summer comfort. Provide now in your construction for a vent at either end of your house.

See section on *Attic Ventilation* for more detailed instructions.

Decide on the final ceiling finish

Before

now, while you are installing the ceiling framing. If you are going to use large boards to finish the ceiling you will have to make provisions for nailing boards. This means you should insert 2x3 or 2x4 lumber at each place where the edges of the sheet must be nailed, including corners. If a vertical plank type finish is to be installed, furring strips, described later, will be needed.

Installing Frame Partitions

If you have included separate rooms with partitions to divide them in your planning this is the next step in your project. The partition walls can be built to run parallel or at right angles to the center ridge board. Use the same size lumber, 2x3's or 2x4's, for the wall studs. Walls that run the length of the attic, parallel to the center ridge board, require a top plate as well as the floor plate.

Cut a 2x4 base plate and partition studs to the proper length, allowing for a top plate to be added later. You can prefabricate your wall partition on the floor of the attic. Tip up your prefabricated assembly in place and nail the base plate to the floor. Make your top plate for the partition, at-

Fiberglas roll blanket insulation may be installed as shown below. Blanket insulation may be nailed or stapled between the wall studs and ceiling joists.

Photograph courtesy Owens-Corning Fiberglas Corp.

After

Photograph courtesy Wood Conversion Co.

After—Another View

tach it to the rafters and nail through it into the top of the vertical partition studs. Built-ins which you have planned should be installed at this time. Be sure to make provisions for the door framing.

Framing a Doorway

Do not install a floor plate in the door frame openings. To determine the proper size for the opening, select your door and check its dimensions.

An attic apartment is a project which can be undertaken inexpensively and take care of the immediate housing needs of the newlyweds or a place for the in-laws.

The overall width of the doorway is the width of the door itself plus 4¾″ to allow for the extra studs and the finished jamb around the door. The overall height is the height of the door plus 1″ if you do not plan to use a threshold, or 2″ if you do.

Also see *DOOR FRAMING*.

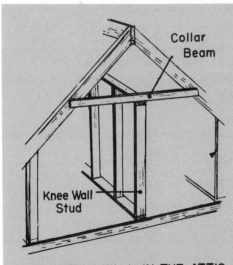

PARTITION WALL IN THE ATTIC

Collar Beam

Knee Wall Stud

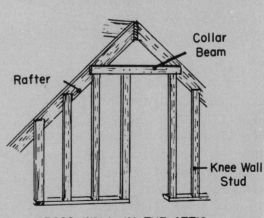

CROSS WALL IN THE ATTIC

Collar Beam

Rafter

Knee Wall Stud

Photograph courtesy Owens-Corning
Fiberglas Corp.

Furring strips must be installed if you plan to use a vertical plank type wall finish. The strips are nailed to studs and joists on all wall and ceiling areas to provide nailing members.

Lighting and Plumbing

Before any more carpentry is done in the attic, now is the time to provide for lighting and plumbing. Local building codes may require that this work be done by an electrician or a plumber.

For wiring details and plumbing techniques and information, see *LIGHTING, WIRING* and *PLUMBING*.

Insulation

Insulating the attic living space is essential not only for added warmth in the winter but to keep out the sun's heat in summer. Three major areas must be insulated for proper efficiency: The floor between the knee-walls and the outside of the house, the end walls, knee-walls and the sloping rafter walls and over the ceiling. You must use an adequate thickness of insulation to keep the rooms comfortable at all times.

There are a number of types of insulating material available: Fiberglas batts or blankets, granule insulation, expandable aluminum foil and others. Follow the manufacturers' instructions for proper installation.

Also see *INSULATION*.

Finishing the Interior

There is a wide variety of attractive and easy-to-install wall materials available. If you plan to use the vertical plank type finish you will have to install 1x2 horizontal furring strips spaced 12″ to 16″ apart. Nail these strips to the studs or joists on all wall and ceiling areas. Be sure to provide a nailing surface on both sides of all angles and corners.

If you decide to use any of the large wallboard materials your job will be easier and faster. Listed here are a number of the materials available and their characteristics.

WALLBOARD (CANE AND FIBRE)—A moderately durable wall surfacing material. Some types come already prefinished. They have good insulating qualities and are moderately soundproof.

WALLBOARD (PRESSED WOOD)—Tough surface is difficult to damage. Made in various finishes and patterns, including perforated and corrugated. Easily painted and moderately priced.

WALLBOARD (PLASTER OR ASBESTOS) — Fire-resistant surfaces. Moderately durable and low in cost. Flat dull surface needs painting or papering. Some now available in simulated wood grains.

PLYWOOD—Strong, with the surface available in different grains and wood species and surface finishes. Takes a permanent finish nicely

Photograph courtesy U.S. Plywood Corp.

and is easily installed. Comes in both panels and planks.

PLASTIC-SURFACED HARD-BOARD)—These prefinished surfaces come in all colors and are easily cleaned. Also available in wood grains and marble effects. Durable surface and moderately priced. Most new types fasten to wall with special concealed hardware and clips or adhesives.

LINOLEUM, VINYL AND RUBBER—Available in rolls of various widths and tiles, Applied to solid wall surfaces with various adhesives. Can

Finish the interior with paint, stain, wallpaper or other decorator's material. The amount of finishing necessary will depend on the material you have used in the construction of your attic rooms.

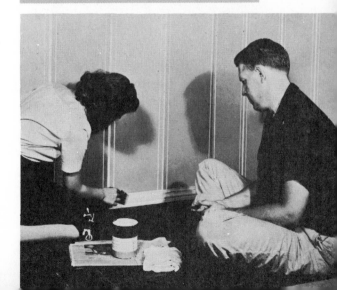

The finished project will give you an extra attractive room like the one shown above. An attic project is low in cost and long on satisfaction.

Photograph courtesy makers of Armstrong's Temlock

be applied to plasterboard and hardboard. Great variety of colors, designs and textures. Easy to maintain and moderately priced.

CORK—Manufactured in tiles 12″ x 12″ or 12″ x 24″. Glued to solid walls or comes already backed on hardboard. Moderately high priced. Good insulator and sound absorber but unless treated, stains easily.

LUMBER—Individual boards and planks, random or selected widths, available in different grains and species. Easily nailed to framing; can be given a permanent natural finish to highlight grain.

The technique used to apply the wall surfacing depends upon the material you have chosen to finish the interior. To install the plank type finish just mentioned after you have nailed up the furring strips, regular or random width 1″ stock boards are nailed with edges butting; use 8-penny finishing or casing nails to attach the planks to ceiling and floor plates, studs and braces. Use a nail set to sink heads of nails below surface. Fill nail holes.

CEMENTING PLYWOOD—Plywood panels, ¼″ thick, are secured with 1½″ long finishing nails into the plates, studs and braces. One of the latest methods of applying plywood walls is with contact cement. The plywood is cemented to the studs, so there is no countersinking nail heads and filling in nail holes before finishing. If you work two sides of the wall at one time there will be no time lost in waiting for the special cement to harden.

The following lists the steps and method of cementing your wall in place:

1. Measure and cut panel to exact size, then lay panel in place and mark location of the studs. When additional panels are to be added the plywood comes to the center of the stud.

2. Work on the reverse side of the plywood and use a straight edge to rule a line corresponding to the center of the studs marked off.

3. Brush an adhesive such as Weldwood Contact Cement over the lines to line up with location of studs. Apply cement liberally.

4. Using the same method, apply cement to the studs. Cement must set for thirty minutes to two hours; on sloping surfaces apply a second coat of the contact cement.

5. Panel is placed in position. With sloping wall installation you will need assistance.

6. Do not apply any pressure

initially, so that you can shift panel slightly to get it perfectly aligned. When properly placed, secure by using hammer and wood block to set cement. The wood block will prevent damage and marks to your panel.

SECURING OTHER WALL SURFACES—Hardboard panels are best secured with 1″ flathead sheet metal screws through pre-drilled holes spaced 8″ apart. Pre-finished hardboard planks and tiles, interlock with tongue-and-groove joints and are held by special metal clips supplied by the manufacturer.

Wallboard can be applied in several different ways. If the surface is to be painted or wallpapered, use 6-penny coated common nails. The new pre-finished panels are also attached with special clips or with 6-penny casing nails set 6″ to 8″ apart.

This attic room took advantage of the extra head room provided by dormers and was used to make a complete attic recreation room including a fully equipped bathroom. The lounges have been designed to be converted into beds as shown.

Linoleum, plastic and rubber tiles must be cemented to the wall. A subgrade of plywood or plaster-board is attached to the studs and braces with nails, setting the nails flush with the surface and cementing the tiles over the rigid wall surface.

CEILING FINISHING—A variety of finishes is available for the ceiling. Depending upon the material you have used for the walls, you may want to cover the ceiling with the same material. The instructions for using the material are basic and the same techniques should be applied. On the other hand, you may wish to

Laying a tile floor in the attic.

Photographs courtesy Bakelite Co.

use a ceiling tile which is available in a number of textures and materials. The installation of tiles for the ceiling is a job that you can tackle by yourself and you can work quickly and efficiently.

The first step in your job will be to square off the room. No matter how careful you were in your framing and wall covering, your ceiling is probably crooked. It will be your task to make the lines formed by the tiles seem square to the casual observer. To do this:

1. Find the center of the room by running a line diagonally across the room from one corner to another and then another line from the other corners of the room.

2. Using a protractor or angle divider, find the center of the angle formed by these diagonals and draw

Photograph courtesy Wood Conversion Co.

Photograph courtesy U.S. Plywood Corp.

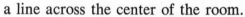

a line across the center of the room.

3. With a framing square draw a line at right angles to the line just drawn.

4. Determine how tiles will come out at the edges by dividing the distance from the center to the wall. Plan placement of the tiles so you do not have narrow edges on both sides of the wall.

To apply the tiles it is necessary to nail 1x3 furring strips at right angles to the ceiling joists with 6-penny common nails. The strips should be nailed 12″ center to center for 12″ tiles or 8″ apart for 16″ tiles. To secure the best results start the tiles at the center of the room and finish one row before you start another.

Also see *CEILING TILES*.

HINTS FOR HANDLING CEILING TILES:

1. For stapling or nailing, put fastener in each flange corner plus 1 staple or nail on flange side of 12″ tiles or two for 16″ tiles.

2. When starting tiles in center of the room, use a nailing strip (T shaped to fit grooves of tiles) or special clips, both available at lumber yards.

3. Attach first row of tiles from wall to wall. Each succeeding row is added from wall to wall before starting on the next row.

4. Score tiles several times with sharp knife or tile cutter on finished side, place over edge of table and snap off sharp edge. Tiles can also be cut with a saw; be sure to keep finished side up.

5. For a neater finish at edges where ceiling tiles meet wall, use a crown moulding. Use a trim to cover tiles brought down to kneewall.

FINISHING THE ATTIC FLOOR—In finishing your attic floor, once again you have a wide variety of materials to choose from. You can install a hardwood floor, linoleum or floor tile, wall to wall carpeting or any one of a dozen other materials depending upon what the rooms are designed for.

Hardwood finish flooring is installed in the same fashion as the tongue and groove subfloor. Never attempt to drive the nails all the way with the hammer. You will break the tongue. Use your nail set to drive the nail the last fraction of an inch. Finish the floor by sanding, staining and varnishing.

Linoleum is installed over a hardboard or plywood underlayment for a smooth finish. If your linoleum is felt-backed you can eliminate the felt padding. Cut the linoleum to fit, apply cement to the floor a few square feet at a time and press linoleum down into the cement. Follow the manufacturers' instructions.

To tile the floor, follow the same procedures for squaring the room as described in Tiling the Ceiling.

The following hints will aid you in doing a professional job.

1. Holes or openings between seams of plywood or subfloor should be filled.

2. Use an underlayment of felt paper base over the floor so that the joints in the subfloor or plywood will not show through.

3. Cut vinyl and rubber tiles with a sharp knife along a straight edge or use a powered jig saw. To cut asphalt tiles to size, score along line with sharp knife; repeat and then snap back from scored line.

4. Eliminate possibilities for error by cutting cardboard patterns for tiles being cut to fit irregular spaces.

5. Tiles should be kept at a 75 degree temperature. For best results warm tiles before laying. The tiles can be warmed near a furnace or heat carefully, using a blowtorch on asphalt tiles.

Before

6. Apply adhesive with a toothed trowel. Flooring paper must show through grooves in the adhesive. After the adhesive has dried for an hour, remark chalk guide lines.

7. The first tile is set on the center of the cross line. Press tight and be careful to use *no* sliding motion.

8. Lay tiles fan-wise over one quarter of the room at a time. Lay all of the tiles in each of the sections except for the section butting against the wall. Follow the manufacturers pattern or design one of your own.

9. Leave ⅛″ for expansion space when you cut the tiles to fit against the baseboard.

ADDING WOOD TRIM—During the course of your carpentry in the attic you have probably made more than a few unsightly joints and made other mistakes here and there. This is where your wood trim serves a dual purpose. While it will add a decorative touch to your project it will also conceal the mistakes. There are a variety of mouldings to choose from and your local lumber dealer will probably have many samples from which you can choose those you prefer.

After

DOOR TRIM—You can probably buy the lumber needed for door framing as a unit at your local lumber yard or purchase the individual moldings. The head jamb is nailed to the header over the door with 8-penny finishing nails. Next attach the side jambs in the same way. These should be 1″ stock boards cut wide enough to cover the edges of the wall material. The next step is to nail the casing, usually 1x4, with mitred corners to jamb and through wall studs so that 3/16″ of jamb is exposed. Attach the door to the jamb and finish by nailing a door stop along the

What was once a dismal, empty garret has been transformed into a lovely guest room, as if by magic. Ceiling tile and false beams give the room a classic look that welcomes visitors.

sides and top with 6-penny finishing nails.

JOINT TRIM—A trim molding is needed to conceal the openings where the ceiling and walls meet and at the junction of walls and floor. It may also be necessary to use a trim molding at the point where the knee-wall ends. The types of molding and their locations are:

1. A crown molding, available in many sizes and styles is used to cover the ceiling-wall joint. Attach with 8-penny finishing nails into studs.

2. Baseboard at the wall-floor joint. This is usually three separate moldings. The baseboard is nailed to the studs with 8-penny finishing nails. A base mold is nailed to the top of that with 6-penny finishing nails. Then for a tight seal along the floor, a shoe mold is used. Window trims are provided with the stock windows purchased.

PAINTING AND DECORATING—Your last step is painting and decorating. Many finish boards do not require paint; if you used any of the pre-finish materials your work has been cut down quite a bit. Paint or stain the trim, depending upon your over-all decorating scheme.Curtains, furniture, lamps and rugs and other incidentals are now ready to be moved in.

Also see *PAINTING* and *WALL-PAPERING*.

STORAGE AREAS—If you had planned on under-eaves storage space here are some hints and suggestions which might prove useful in your planning. There are generally two ways to handle the unusual storage space provided by the under-eaves. One is a corner closet and the other is shallow storage units.

The corner areas adjoining a shed dormer are difficult to incorporate as part of your attic living space. In this space you can readily make a side or front entrance closet for clothing or storage. Whether you decide to make a front entrance or side entrance closet, it will be necessary to:

1. Frame around the perimeter, constructing studs as you would normally do for partition walls.

2. A double stud must be erected on both sides of the door opening and a double header fits across the top of the opening. In the case of the side opening closet the header is cut at an angle to match the slope of the rafter.

3. Use a solid core flush door cut to size for the side entrance closet, or make one from 1x3's sandwiched between two pieces of ¼" plywood.

4. The door is attached with hinges and a door pull and catch or any standard door hardware.

5. The front entrance closet door can be made in the same manner as the side entrance closet or use ¾" plywood.

6. Attach closet hardware such as poles, hooks, racks or other, depending upon the items to be stored.

Shallow storage units are especially suitable for attics with low knee-walls and shallow under the eaves storage space. You can construct the storage space with sliding doors or open shelves or even drawers built into the walls.

Before

Extra play space and children's room— attractive and easy to clean—was constructed in an attic where hundreds of square feet of space were being wasted.

Photograph courtesy Wood Conversion Co.

The following steps will help you organize and work out your project.

1. After you have decided where and what type of built-in you need, leave an opening in the knee-wall and do not set any studs in place. Cut two short studs and attach them to the rafter and a floor plate at the rear of the storage space. They will form the other three sides of your built-in.

2. Across the rafters in this space add any wall surfacing material to seal off the built-in from side to side and from the front edge of the unit to the short studs in the back.

3. A quick, easy way to add shelf space, if it is to be covered with sliding doors, is to build a framed unit of ⅜″ or ½″ plywood. The shelves are attached by #8 flathead screws and the back is formed of hardboard or plywood. This unit is slid into place

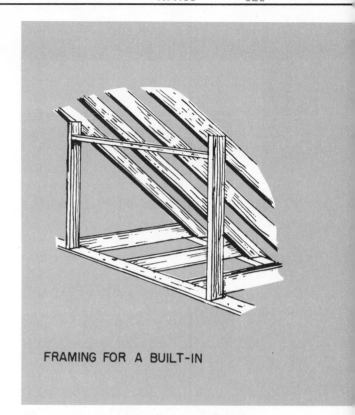

FRAMING FOR A BUILT-IN

After

and a front baseboard is attached, if the unit is to be left open.

4. If you plan to conceal the unit behind sliding doors, make the entire unit as described but make it 1½" less than the depth of the under-eaves closet to allow for the doors and track.

5. You can also turn the open shelves into drawers. Make the basic frame as described and drawers to fit into this. Follow the proportions suggested here for ease of handling and appearance.

a. If the drawer is less than 4 inches deep it can be made up to 18" wide.

b. If the drawer is between 4" and 7" deep, the maximum width should be no more than 14".

c. If the drawer is up to 12" deep, make it no more than 12" wide.

6. From ½" plywood cut two sides and the front and back panels. Join these pieces with #6 flathead screws 1¼" long, countersinking heads. Space these screws at least 3" apart, using three to each corner.

7. Cut ½"x½" cleats to fit inside this frame flush with the bottom edge. Hold the cleats to the sides with #6 flathead screws ¾" long, spaced 2" apart with countersunk heads.

8. The bottom of the drawer fits inside this frame and rests on the cleats. Cut the drawer bottoms from ¼" plywood; secure with brads.

9. Faceplate of drawers, made of ¾" plywood, is cut to extend ¼" on all sides.

10. Secure the face plate to front panel by screws from inside of drawer. Use #6 flathead screws 1" long spaced about 4" apart along the top and bottom. Countersink heads.

CLOSETS IN THE ATTIC—

While on the subject of attic storage space you may want to consider dividing the attic with closet walls. You can make the walls functional by turning them into closets and the use of sliding doors will also save you valuable space. Constructing a closet wall begins in the same manner as erecting a wall. Plates and studs are nailed in position with an opening left for doors.

1. First complete the basic framing, then cut two studs to door height plus depth of sliding door hardware plus an additional ½" for clearance.

2. Nail these two studs to both sides of the opening with 10-penny nails. Cut a door header from two pieces of lumber, same dimensions as studs, long enough to rest on studs cut in previous step.

3. Nail both pieces together and toe-nail in place resting on studs.

4. If you make two closets back-to-back, add a divider wall between them of hardboard or utility grade plywood.

5. Add shelves to suit and clothes pole. The clothes pole, a 1½" or 2" dowel or metal rod, should be at least 63" above the floor for adults and about 45" for children.

6. Mount the sliding door hardware on the underside of the door header.

7. Buy two doors or make them from ¾" plywood or Novoply allowing 1" overlap in the center and about ¼" clearance above the floor plate.

8. Secure hardware to the doors and lift into place. The wall surfacing material is applied over framing and exposed surfaces and decorative trim is added around the door and joints.

Also see *BUILT-INS*.

Before

A girl's room for study and entertainment was constructed in this attic where formerly leftovers and broken furniture took up valuable space.

After

TWO NOVEL ATTIC TREATMENTS

Planned for easy maintenance, this finished attic room for two young teen boys leaves nothing to be desired. Floors are covered with washable Armstrong Corlon, and walls are finished in flat enamel. This open plan, without confining walls, adds spaciousness as no other plan can.

For the younger set, the campsite atmosphere so artfully generated will keep kids happy. The trees are real. They are cut to length and wedged in place. Note work-study area at far right.

Photos courtesy Armstrong Cork. Co.

ADDING A DORMER—If your attic ceiling is so low that you cannot make efficient use of the attic space the chances are that you will have to raise the ceiling of the attic by constructing a dormer. The two types of dormers most commonly used are gable and shed. A gable dormer usually provides only one window and is generally constructed in attics which have sufficient headroom but little light. A shed dormer raises the entire roof line of a house except at the ridge.

Building a dormer is the hardest part of reconverting an attic and you may want to hire a professional carpenter. If, however, you feel that you can tackle a project such as this the following suggestions and hints will help you to organize and carry out this project.

SHED DORMER

1. Take a snapshot or make a sketch of your house and indicate where the dormer will go. Plan for a height of 7'6" and a length suitable for your attic project. Remember that a dormer should begin and end at a rafter.

2. Make a scale drawing of the dormer, showing every framing member in place. From this you can estimate the materials needed. Figure area of walls and roof to be covered by 1x8 sheathing and add about 20% for scrap.

3. First cut along the inside of the rafters down to the top plate on which the rafters rest. Start your cuts in a drilled hole and use a keyhole saw. The sawed boards are knocked loose from inside the attic.

4. Doubled corner studs are set up first and nailed to both top plate and to rafters which will later be cut.

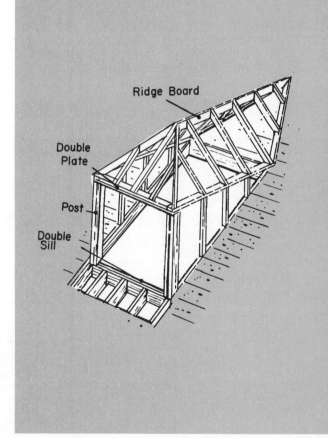

Check carefully with carpenter's level to make sure studs are vertical.

5. Frame the windows with double 2x4's set on edge across the top and a single 2x4 flat on the bottom. Six 10d nails are used to toenail each stud to plate. At this point your window opening will depend upon the style and amount of windows you plan for the dormer.

6. Nail 1x6 blocks on opposing rafters to support 16 foot 2x6 stringers. Toe-nail stringers to new top plate with 8d nails.

7. Across the top edge of the new

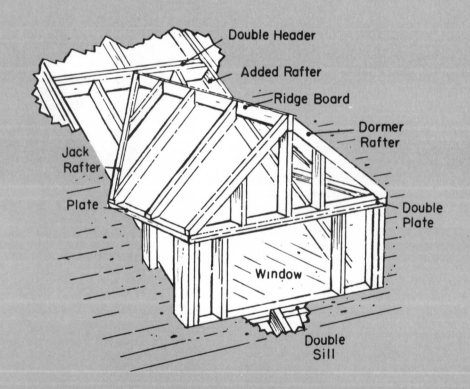

Double Header

Added Rafter

Ridge Board

Dormer Rafter

Jack Rafter

Plate

Double Plate

Window

Double Sill

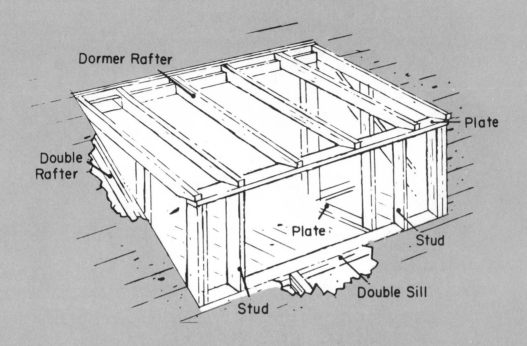

Dormer Rafter

Double Rafter

Plate

Plate

Stud

Stud

Double Sill

opening nail a 1x6. Set rafters in place and toe-nail with 8d nails to the 1x6 at the top end, and to the stringers at the other end.

8. After the new rafters are set in their proper positions, the old ones should be cut flush with the new studs and the stringers. Then remove the old ones. Nail 2x6's between stringers onto plates.

9. Starting at the front edge of the roof, put roof sheathing across the rafters.

10. Use 15# felt to cover the roof. Carry the first strip down over the stringer ends to underside. Cover the underside of the dormer roof with 1/4" exterior grade plywood. Nail a 1x6 fascia board across.

11. Cover the felt with roll roofing, starting at the fascia. The overlap of strips is 2" and use roofing adhesive along seams and to coat the nail heads.

12. Cut metal flashings and insert 6" under old roofing and 8" out over last strip of new roofing. Coat this flashing liberally with roofing compound along the edges.

13. Use 1x8 sheathing for front

and side walls. Cut the board ends at the angle of the roof pitch to fit flush against the roof.

14. The side sheathing is covered with felt, starting at the bottom and overlapping 4″ over roof in front and at the sides.

15. Stock window frames are toe-nailed into the openings provided for them. Use your carpenter's level to make sure you have them in the proper position.

16. Metal flashing is run 6″ up the side and front walls and 4″ over roof all around. The siding is butted against the window casing. Rest the siding on the flashing.

17. Blanket insulation is applied between ceiling joists and between outer wall studs. Staple insulation back from front of studs to provide dead air space.

18. Finish the interior the same as the rest of the attic.

19. The exterior is finished with sheathing, shingles or other material to match the rest of the house.

Interior construction details are explained in this section on attics. Individual projects such as plumbing, wiring, and heating are explained in the sections under appropriate subject headings.

Also see *BUILT-INS, CEILING TILES, FLOORS, WALLS* and *WIRING*.

This attic space was designed to provide room for a guest room, a place where the family can relax and a child's room. Here the chimney which ran up through the second floor, was painted white and a Franklin stove was piped into it.

Photograph courtesy makers of Armstrong's Linoleum

Auger

Commonly called a "snake," an auger is used to clear blocked pipes. There are many different types, ranging from flat spring steel with a twisted wire hook at the forward end to spiral-wound heavy steel wire with a handle.

Also see *PLUMBING* and *PIPES*.

Auger Bit

Auger bits are used only in wood working for boring holes. They are used with a brace and are sized by 16th of an inch. These bits are available in sizes ranging from ¾₁₆″ to 1″ and vary in length from 7″ to 10″. Short auger bits, about 5″ long, are technically called dowel bits.

There are two types of auger bits: single and double twist. For fast boring, use a single twist auger. It has only one spur and cutting edge. The double twist type, which has two spurs and cutting lips, is better for smooth boring, especially when doing fine cabinet work with seasoned wood.

Use a bit file to sharpen an auger bit. Be certain to sharpen the spurs on the inside in order to preserve the diameter of the bit.

Sharpen the cutting edges of the top to maintain the clearance on the underside.

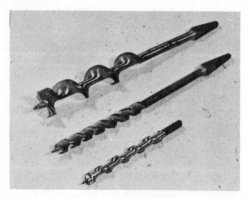

Auger bits with their feed screws and spurs are made for use with a brace or a hand or electric drill. The tapered tang or end of the bit (upper two bits in photograph) fit the chuck of a brace. The bit (bottom) is used with a hand or, preferably, with an electric drill.

The Basic Parts of an Auger Bit

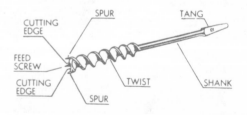

CUTTING EDGE   SPUR   TANG

FEED SCREW

CUTTING EDGE   SPUR   TWIST   SHANK

Sketches from "Tool Guide" courtesy of Stanley Tools, Division of The Stanley Works

Awl

A small pointed tool used for making pilot holes for nails or screws. It is particularly useful in making pilot holes for brads, or small nails, when exact position is necessary.

The awl in many ways serves the same function as a small drill bit but the hole it makes becomes larger in diameter as the point is forced into the wood.

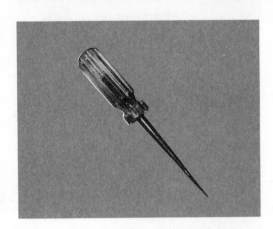

Awnings

The life of awnings may be prolonged with periodic inspection, care, and proper storage. Inspect the awnings when they are taken down in the fall, make all repairs necessary, so that next spring when they are again needed they will be in good condition.

Cleaning

Just before taking down, while awnings are still on the window, remove all dust with a stiff dry brush. Then dip the brush in a solution of lukewarm water and mild soap suds, and wash the awning. Remove soap suds with a clean cloth wrung out in clear lukewarm water. Let awnings remain open until thoroughly dry. Then take them down.

Repairing

If there are any frayed cords they should be replaced now. If the metal framework or the pulleys are rusted, or don't work easily, now is the time to remove the rust, to paint the frame-work, and oil the pulleys.

Any holes in the awning should be patched now. Use a rubber cement or other special glue which is obtainable at the hardware store, and attach the patch with this adhesive on the outside of the awning. Be sure to cut the patch about an inch bigger than the hole all around.

Painting

Use canvas paint. Hang the awning on the lowest window of your house; let the awning down, and paint it with long, even strokes. Do the entire job at once; if you try to do it in two days there might be streaks where you left off the first day. If your awning is striped, choose a paint to match the darker color of the stripe. The awning must remain opened until the paint is thoroughly dry.

Storing

The awning must be cleaned and

Canvas panels, laced on metal frames made of aluminum tubing or pipe, are supported by upright pipes anchored to the concrete patio and secured to the edge of the roof. Used as a patio roof and as vertical shields to an overhang, the awnings give this contemporary home a bright new look.

repaired before it is packed away for the cold weather. It must be thoroughly dry, to prevent any danger of mildew. Fold the awning, cover it with heavy wrapping paper or a piece of canvas, and store it in a dry spot. If it needs painting, it is best to wait until you unwrap it next spring, and do the job at that time.

How to Make a Fixed Awning

You can keep Old Sol from beating through the windows in the summer and make your home a much cooler place in which to live. Permanent awnings not only are attractive but they have a cooling function as well.

There are several advantages to making your own. Constructing the awning shown in the accompanying sketches is simple and it is cheaper than purchasing ready-made. You may paint this type of awning any color you wish.

Each awning should have a simple framework of 1 x 2 dressed lumber with cross-pieces 16″ apart. It should be covered with building panel that will last as long as the house. Masonite's Tempered Presdwood, either ¼″ or ³⁄₁₆″, will do that job. The panels may form a solid cover over the framework, or they may be cut into strips 4″ to 6″ wide and nailed to the framework with small spaces, about ¼″ to ⅜″, between each strip.

If strips are used, use pieces of tempered hardboard of the same width under the framing too, spacing them to cover the openings above in the slanting portion of the awning.

If the solid-type covering is used, provide a couple of vent slots at the top of the awning to permit the escape of heated air.

Finish the awning with a good primer and two finish coats of a quality exterior type of paint. Use of

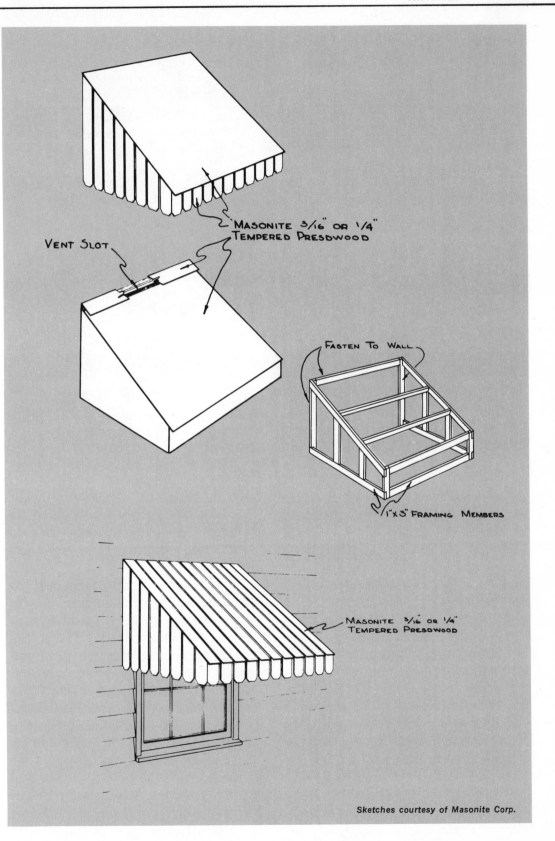

MASONITE 3/16" OR 1/4"
TEMPERED PRESDWOOD

VENT SLOT

FASTEN TO WALL

1"x3" FRAMING MEMBERS

MASONITE 3/16" OR 1/4"
TEMPERED PRESDWOOD

Sketches courtesy of Masonite Corp.

You can stay on friendly terms with the sun all summer long if you have a canvas-covered patio. An iron pipe or aluminum framework is covered with canvas awning to produce cool and comfortable shade outdoors and inside as well.

different colors on alternating strips of the awning will produce a pleasing effect.

Awnings of this type will keep the inside temperature of your home from 5 to 10 degrees cooler on a scorching day.

Canvas Awning Projects

Cotton canvas, traditionally used for awnings, can help you live with the hot summer sun and like it. With this heavy fabric at your windows and doorways, your rooms will remain cool and comfortable despite high thermometer readings.

To stay on friendly terms with Old Sol, you need effective and flexible protection on all sides of your home.

In addition to overheating your rooms, the summer sun is likely to damage colors in your draperies, rugs and fabric-covered couches and chairs.

Whether you have standard or floor-to-ceiling windows, canvas awnings can be designed to solve your particular sun problems. They will keep indoor temperatures down and interior furnishings fresh and unfaded by effectively screening 75% of the solar rays. As soon as the sun changes its course or sets in the evening, cotton canvas awnings can be raised to let cool air enter your rooms.

Even if your house is air conditioned, your windows need to be protected from the sun. Recent studies show that glass lets in 35 times as much solar heat as an insulated wall. By intercepting the sun's rays, canvas awnings will reduce the cooling load on your air conditioning units and save money on their operation.

If you're tired of that closed-in feeling, use canvas to expand your home for modern summer living. With a window wall and connecting terrace, you can double the space and livability of a room and open the way to pleasant outdoor entertaining and relaxing. A wide sweep of colorful canvas over the terrace will shade both indoor and outdoor areas.

If you have a window wall and no terrace, outside draw draperies of canvas will give you protection and privacy at a moment's notice. They will keep the sun in its place when necessary and allow you to invite nature indoors at other times of the day.

Canvas panels laced on metal frames and hinged to an overhang can contribute to your summer comfort in two ways. The panels may be extended horizontally as a patio roof or dropped to hang vertically in front of your windows. A movable roof operated by pulleys will provide a shady spot by day and a cool open area by night.

Your awnings can be flattering additions to your house. You will find canvas in a myriad of gay solid hues and rainbow stripes. To rigid glass and wood or stone sidings, the heavy cotton fabric offers a bright and texturally-interesting contrast.

Like colored frosting on a cake, canvas can be the final decorative touch enhancing the eye-appeal of

This attractive overhang awning to shade the windows of the house and protect the walk in rainy weather, can be made by lacing canvas awning to a rigid iron or aluminum frame. The uprights are set into the ground, preferably into concrete, 8″ in diameter and about 12″ deep.

Sketches courtesy of National Cotton Council

Old Sol traveling through the sky may strike at this western exposure in the late afternoon. But you won't have to worry about that if you have a vertical roller awning teamed with a wide roof overhang. The awning can be mounted on a shade roller or worked on a pulley system so that it moves up and down freely.

Pivot sun screens are practically a copy of the Venetian blinds you might have on your windows. It's easier to make these metal frames out of Do-It-Yourself Aluminum, but the more advanced handyman can try to do this with pipe. A tight fit into the flanges in the roof and floor will keep the sun screens moving in the breeze.

Photos and sketches courtesy of
National Cotton Council

your house. A wise color choice will complement other elements making up the exterior. You may want to repeat the hue of your roof or match your sun shades to painted shutters and doors. Whatever color recipe you use, canvas will mix well with the other ingredients.

Here's one way to keep the sun from being an unwelcome house guest in the summer. Outside draw draperies keep the sun in its place when necessary but open the way for enjoyable indoor-outdoor living at other times of the day. They are hung on a conventional draw-drape rod, but make certain the hardware is rustproof.

You can't change the weather outdoors but you can do something about your own private climate inside and surrounding your home. Canvas at your windows and doorways, and over your patio or terrace, can help you enjoy a cooler and happier summer. Awnings of this versatile fabric will not only protect your home from the sun's glare but give it new beauty.

There are many different ways in which you can use canvas awnings to sun-control your indoor and outdoor living. Here are a few for the handyman to build and make his outdoor living more enjoyable.

Baby Protectors

For the active child in the crawling and toddling stage, protection must be provided at open windows, doorways, porches, and stairways.

Open Porch Railings

Where the upright spokes in the porch railing are spaced widely apart, it is wise to put a screened "fence" inside the railing. This can be ordinary screen wire, either tacked on a frame attached to the inside of the railings, or nailed directly over the railings.

Stairways and Doorways

The folding safety gate, which can be bought at any hardware store, is the best thing to use at the top of a stairway, or at doorways through which you do not want the child to wander. Installation is a simple procedure; the gate may be screwed to one wall, the latch to the opposite wall. It is very easy for the adult to manipulate yet is out of reach of the child.

Windows

The simplest way to keep the window covered is a wire screen fixed to the window frame. (The sliding screens may prove a hazard to the child's curious and busy fingers.) Or, if you do not wish to keep the screen in permanently, nail wood spokes either horizontally or vertically into the window frame, the spokes spaced closely together so the child cannot go through.

Back Fill

This term has several meanings for the home handyman. It can be used to describe the rubble or soil thrown in behind a retaining wall: It can also be used to designate the rough masonry built behind the facing or between two faces or surfaces. In bricklaying, it is used to describe any brickwork used to fill in the space between studs in a frame or wooden building.

Backfire

This is an automotive term used to describe an intake or exhaust explosion taking place in a car's passages. It may be caused by faulty valves, late timing or a lean fuel mixture. Instead of igniting in the cylinder, the fuel explodes in the manifold and you hear a sharp noise.

Also see *CARS*.

Backsaw

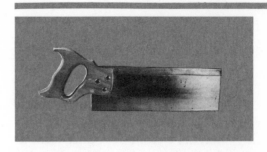

This saw gets its name from the heavy piece of steel which is secured to the back of the blade to reinforce and stiffen it. The teeth are cross-cut and fine, varying from 8 to 16 per inch, the most commonly used having 14 points, or teeth, per inch. The backsaw is often used in a miter box for fine, accurate cutting, like that required in making wood joints.

When working with a backsaw, always start with a short, light stroke toward you, with the handle raised slightly above the work. Continue with light strokes, gradually lowering the handle until the saw is cutting on a horizontal plane.

Also see *SAWS*.

Baffle

A loudspeaker generates sound waves in two directions—from the front and the back. A baffle is used with a loudspeaker to separate these two sound waves. It is designed to act as a partition or barrier to help the tone response of the loudspeaker.

Also see *HI-FI* and *FOLDED HORN*.

1. An "infinite baffle" is merely a totally enclosed box with a circular hole in the front, behind which the speaker is mounted. It is considered by experts as one of the best ways to mount a speaker. However, the size box needed for most speakers is too large to place in the home.

2. A "bass reflex" enclosure also acts as a baffle for a speaker. It is exceedingly popular and very simple for the handyman to make. Not only is there a circular opening behind which the speaker is mounted, but there is a port opening, a rectangular hole, below the speaker mounting hole.

3. A "folded horn" is another variation of a baffle. It is a complex enclosure for which detailed plans are needed. The handyman must have not only great skill but a number of power tools to do an effective job in making a unit of this type. A folded horn should be placed in a corner of a room.

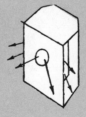

Ball Pein Hammer

The ball pein hammer is the "mechanic's" hammer. It is used for chipping, for example, with a cold chisel, for flattening rivets and for shaping metal. These hammers come in varying weights—from 4 ounces to 2 pounds. Which weight you select depends upon the job being done and your own preference.

Using a Ball Pein Hammer

The ball pein hammer is used much in the same way as the conventional hammer with which all handymen are familiar. Like the regular hammer, the two ends of a ball pein hammer are used for different purposes as noted in the accompanying sketches.

To strike a heavy or medium blow with a ball pein hammer, grasp hammer firmly near the end of handle and swing it with a free, graceful sweep, well over the shoulder.

To strike light blows, as in driving rivets, grasp the handle nearer the head and swing with a motion slightly at the elbow but chiefly at the wrist.

Safety When Using

Like any tool, certain safety precautions must be observed when using. The hammer is no more dangerous than the conventional hammer, but unless used properly, the handyman can mar the work or possibly wind up with a sore thumb.

Here are several basic rules to follow when using a ball pein hammer:

1. Inspect the hammer every time you take it from your tool rack. Be certain that the head is firmly attached and that the wedges holding the head in place are driven tightly into the head and handle.

2. Avoid striking the handle to save it from breakage.

3. Avoid chipping the edges of the hammer face, especially when striking hard metals.

4. Avoid striking with the cheek

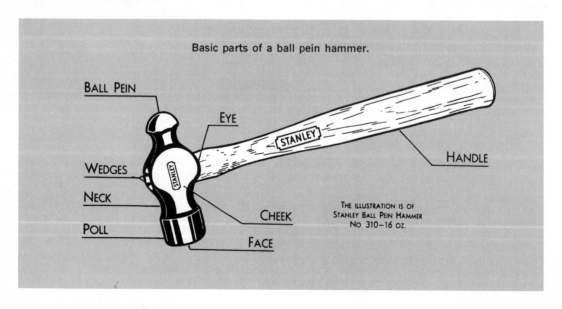

Basic parts of a ball pein hammer.

BALL PEIN

EYE

WEDGES

NECK

POLL

CHEEK

FACE

HANDLE

STANLEY

THE ILLUSTRATION IS OF
STANLEY BALL PEIN HAMMER
NO 310-16 OZ.

or side of the hammer head as this is its weakest part.

Types of Ball Pein Hammers

In addition to the standard ball pein hammer, there are straight and cross pein hammers. The latter are used for specialized metal work. If you do a considerable amount of metal work in your workshop, you will undoubtedly want to have all types of pein hammers available. The average handyman, however, has little use for the straight or cross pein hammers.

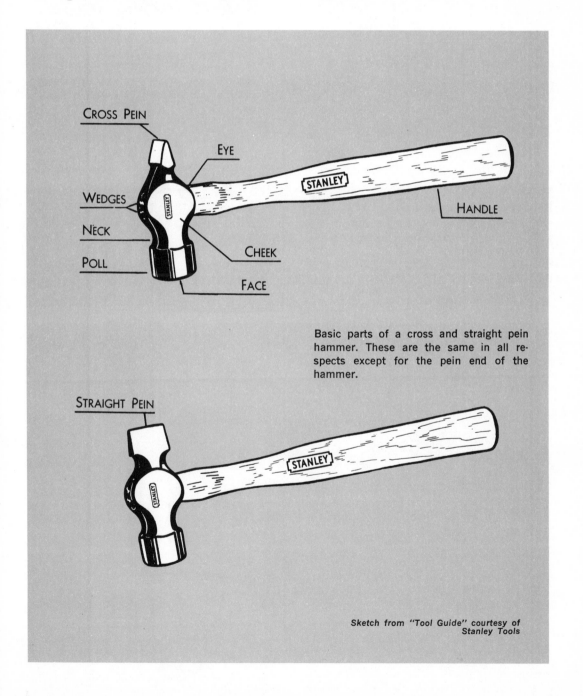

Basic parts of a cross and straight pein hammer. These are the same in all respects except for the pein end of the hammer.

Sketch from "Tool Guide" courtesy of Stanley Tools

To rivet with a ball pein hammer, support the rivet on something hard, like a stake or a block of metal and draw the parts together with a rivet set or with a drift. Strike down on the rivet with the ball pein. Then head the rivet over, that is spread it out so that the top exposed end is larger in diameter than the hole through which the rivet passed. Use either the ball pein or the face of the hammer.

If you have used a center punch to mark the starting place for drilling through metal and the punch mark is in the wrong place, hammer out the old mark with the ball pein.

For many metal working jobs, a ball pein hammer may not be suitable, for example, for bending metal at a right angle. Use a cross pein or straight pein hammer for the job instead.

To stretch a piece of metal stock in the direction of its width, use a cross pein.

To stretch a piece of metal stock in the direction of its length, use a straight pein.

Sketch from "Tool Guide" courtesy of Stanley Tools

Baluster

The vertical supports used to hold a hand rail on a stairway are called balusters.

Also see *STAIRS*.

Band Saw

The blade of this power saw consists of an endless, flexible steel band, with teeth cut on one edge. It revolves about two vertical pulleys or wheels, and is inserted through a hole in the horizontal table on which the cutting is done. The band saw is used for cutting curved edges or combinations of straight and curved work. Many saws have a table that can be tilted 45° making bevel cuts possible.

The size of a band saw is measured by the diameter of the wheel; thus a saw with 10″ wheels would be called a 10″ saw. It can be mounted on a steel stand or wood bench, with the saw table about 43″ from the floor. For the home handyman a ⅓ H.P. motor will be strong enough. It should be a constant-speed, 1725 r.p.m. motor.

The operation of a band saw is relatively safe and simple and even an amateur can turn out a creditable piece of work. The most important precaution is to keep the blade sharp, since a dull blade requires greater feeding pressure with more tendency for the hand to slip.

Also see *SAWS*.

This band saw features a tilting mechanism permitting the handyman to do angle cutting. Note clamp guide and saw blade guard which protects the handyman when using the band saw.

Compact three-wheel band saw capable of cutting thin plywood to heavy 2x4's. The under blade capacity (below the blade and clamp guides) is 3¼″. Comes with blower-cooled, built-in motor so that there's no need for pulleys or belts.

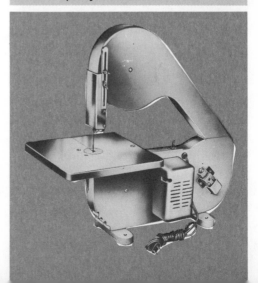

Banisters

Aside from the safety factor of a banister along the stairway, it should also be attractive and fit in with the decorating scheme of your house. If you feel that the existing banister is out-dated, replace it by building or buying one of more modern design.

In an enclosed stairway, or one leading to the basement or attic, there may be no banister or handrail. You could easily remedy the omission by a rope extended the full length of the stairway. Fasten to the wall either wooden or metal rings, spaced about three feet apart. Pull the rope through these rings and it acts as a handrail. The rope should be thick and smooth (no splintering). To make it more decorative, paint the rope (using a canvas paint) to match or contrast with the wall; or you might even sew a "slipcover" of a sturdy material to slide over the rope.

Also see *STAIRS*.

Bar Clamp

A bar clamp has two metal jaws, one of which is actuated by a screw while the other remains in a fixed position. Actually, there are two types of bar clamps used by the handyman. One is the professional type model used in the furniture trade which has two jaws secured to a flat metal bar, and the other, more commonly used by the handyman, has two metal jaws which ride on a pipe.

The pipe type of bar clamp has many advantages for the home handyman because its length is determined by the length of the pipe used. The professional bar clamp comes in many different sizes but is impossible to make longer. With a pipe clamp, however, the handyman can replace the existing pipe with a longer piece should he find it necessary. The most popular pipe clamp has for its bar a ¾" pipe, which you can buy in any hardware store in whatever lengths you desire. The pipe plus the two metal jaws costs about one-half the price of the standard bar type.

Bar clamps are used to hold large pieces of wood together while they are being assembled or until the glue has dried. It is advisable for the handyman to have several pairs of pipe clamps in his workshop together with extra pipe in assorted lengths so that he can put together the right size clamp when he needs it.

Also see *ADHESIVES* and *CLAMPS*.

Barbecue

The outdoor fireplace is popularly referred to as the "barbecue." An outdoor fireplace and picnic area are now part of many home grounds as they provide entertainment and recreation for the family and their friends.

In planning a picnic area, the location of the fireplace, with its picnic furnishings, and the design and construction, are most important. Some fireplaces are elaborate and therefore costly; but these are not necessarily the best unless the surroundings demand one of intricate design. A simple low-cost fireplace can be fitted into a carefully planned scheme.

Location of Fireplace

The possible locations for a fireplace vary with the property on which it is to be constructed. It may be near the house or the garage or at some more distant place. A fireplace may be built onto the outside of a house chimney. Its flue should have a damper or be plugged in winter to prevent any interference with the draft in the flue of the home heating plant. The

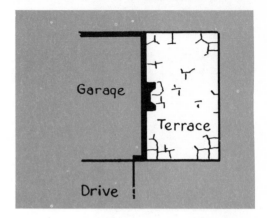

1. You can build your barbecue so that it is against the wall of your garage. However, provide a high chimney to keep the smoke away from your terrace or patio.

2. The barbecue can be built at one end of a terrace on a narrow lot. This will provide you with sufficient seating room away from the fire when the weather is too hot.

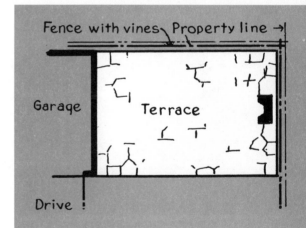

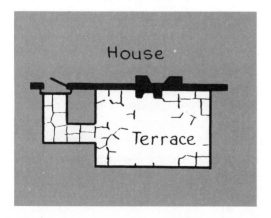

3. If your fireplace chimney in the house has a large enough flue or space for an added flue, you can build your outdoor fireplace up against the same wall and have it use the same chimney as your interior fireplace. But better check the flue to see if it can handle both before you start working on this project.

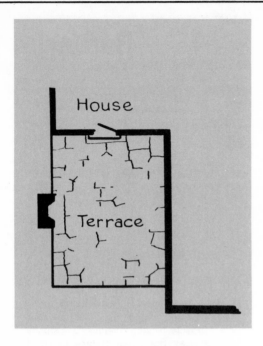

4. Here's another variation for building an outdoor fireplace. It can be built parallel with a house wall forming an attractive sitting area on the rectangular terrace.

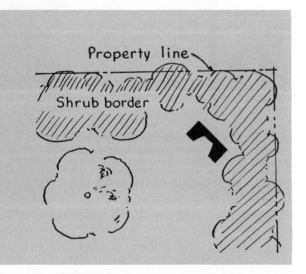

5. If you want to keep the cooking away from your home and you have a large lot, build that barbecue in a corner near the property line.

barbecue should not be near a frame building because of the fire hazard. Any local fire regulations must be observed. If the house is of stone, brick, or asbestos-shingle siding, the fire-hazard is not so great.

An outdoor fireplace near the house is convenient for carrying food and utensils from the house.

In more informal developments and where more space is available, the fireplace should have an adequate background of foliage. A fireplace without a chimney should face the prevailing winds so the smoke will be blown away from the cook and the table. A shade tree at the west or southwest of the picnic area provides shade for the table and chairs.

If the slope of the ground in front of the fireplace is such that furniture cannot be comfortably used, some grading and construction should be done.

Provide a level area for the furniture, and make enclosing walls high enough, about 16″ to 20″ above the floor of the terrace, to be used as seats at the table. The fireplace may be put in a natural grove of trees.

Fire Hazard

The fire hazard is not great, particularly if near-by buildings are fireproof or if the barbecue is about 50′ from the nearest building. One seldom builds a roaring fire, for a fire burned down to coals provides the best cooking heat. Wood that crackles and snaps should not be used. A charcoal fire is excellent. Someone usually is near-by all the time the fire is burning and quick action can be taken in any emergency. The fire usually burns out of its own accord before the meal is over or soon after, but before leaving be sure that it is completely out.

Construction Material

Barbecues may be made of brick or stone or a combination of both. It is more difficult to obtain good results with round field stone than with flat stones, such as limestone. The firebox should be made of firebrick or of a highly glazed brick, because most types of stone crack or "explode" if submitted to intense heat. The foundation is made of concrete: 1 part of cement, 2 parts of sand, and 3 parts of gravel. A small fireplace with or without a chimney needs only a concrete slab from 4″ to 6″ thick and reinforced with old wire or metal rods. A larger fireplace, especially one with a chimney attached to a building, should have a foundation that extends about 42″ below the soil level or below the frost line. One sack of cement, 2 cubic feet of sand, and 3 cubic feet of gravel, will make about 3 to 3½ cubic feet of concrete. Three parts of sand and one part of cement are mixed into a mortar and used for the walls and the firebox.

Special metal grates are sometimes used, but adequate parts may be made from old pipes or metal sheets. The top section of an old wood or coal-burning kitchen range could be used. This assembly sometimes includes a reservoir for heating water.

Construction Plans

None of the plans shown need be followed exactly. The drawings merely illustrate the different types of outdoor fireplaces. Materials that

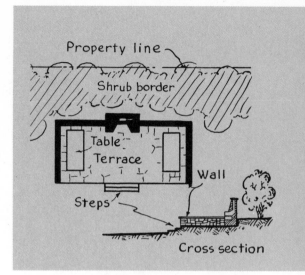

6. If your property slopes, it's better to build the barbecue on the higher ground than at the lower level. You will encounter less difficulty with smoke in this way.

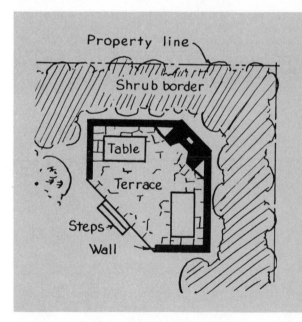

7. Spacious outdoor living is yours on a large lot. Build your patio and the barbecue as its central focal point on the corner of your property. You can have your privacy by planting large shrubs on both sides facing your neighbors.

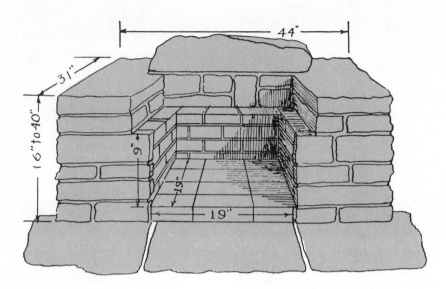

8. Details of a wood-burning fireplace made of stones and firebrick, used at the base. The amateur handyman should not attempt to build a stone barbecue until he has had sufficient experience in working with concrete and stone. See related masonry sections in these volumes for basic how-to.

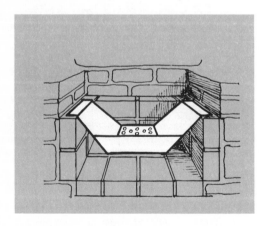

9. A shelf, or grate, can be used if you want to use charcoal in a wood-burning fireplace. You can purchase these grates in some hardware stores or make one out of sheet metal. Remove it during the winter or else it will rust and you'll have to buy a new one for next summer.

are in harmony with the surroundings and those most conveniently available should be used.

A wood-burning fireplace usually has a firebox about 19″ square and 9″ high; the height and depth should not vary much from these dimensions. The length of the firebox and the outside dimensions can vary with the size of the available grates and according to your own desire. The shelves on each side of the grate should be large enough to set dishes and food near the cooking surface. The firebox is built first and then the shelf space.

Charcoal makes the best fire for cooking. A charcoal shelf or grate may be bent to fit a wood-burning fireplace. This can be made from a sheet of metal (28″ by 18″ for a 19-inch square firebox). Light-weight metal can be supported from underneath with bricks to prevent warping or bending. The depth of this adaptor, or grate, should be about 5″, and the sides should slope as shown. The bottom level is about 8″ wide. With the sloping sides and shallow depth, this conserves fuel and gives a good cooking heat. The front edge should have a low siding to keep the coals from falling on the hearth.

When charcoal only is used for fuel, it is better to build a fireplace for this purpose. The distance from the fine-mesh grate on which the charcoal is placed to the cooking grate above should be about 5″. Both grates may be larger than indicated if a larger cooking surface is desired. The grate should be closer to the front than to the back, so it will be easy to reach the cooking surface.

An elaborate fireplace with a chimney may include not only a wood storage box but warming ovens, grills, places to store outdoor furniture and many other special features that add to its usefulness. Shelves on the chimney are convenient for salt-and-pepper shakers, cooking spoons, forks, and small pans.

Unless large fires are built, the chimney need not be lined with flue tile. Such lining, however, is desirable as most stones and soft brick crack when subjected to sudden intense heat.

The floor of the wood box should slope, so water cannot stand and keep the wood wet.

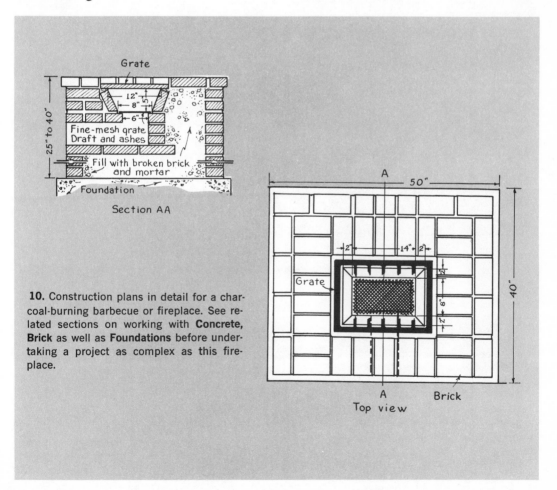

10. Construction plans in detail for a charcoal-burning barbecue or fireplace. See related sections on working with **Concrete, Brick** as well as **Foundations** before undertaking a project as complex as this fireplace.

Easy-to-Build Barbecue

This deluxe barbecue is easily made by any handyman, even those who have never "buttered" a concrete block before. The total time is just two Saturdays: one to prepare and pour the base and the next (allowing time for the concrete base to harden) to erect the structure. Actually, it takes only two days to build this unit, but since curing of concrete cannot be rushed by the handyman, it's best to spread this job out over two weekends.

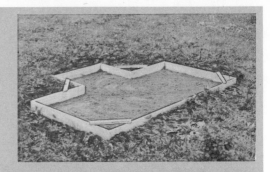

1. Using stakes, mark out the area to be covered by your barbecue. Dig out this area to a depth of 12″. Now fill this opening to within 2″ of the top with gravel or crushed stone. Using 2x4 lumber, nail a form together so that it extends 2″ above the ground level along the perimeter of the opening.

2. Mix a batch of concrete—1 part Portland cement, 2½ parts clean sand and 5 parts gravel, plus water. Pour 2″ of concrete, until level with the ground and then spread some heavy wire or hardware cloth across the opening. Now add 2″ more of concrete and level it smooth with top of form.

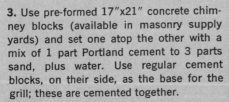

3. Use pre-formed 17″x21″ concrete chimney blocks (available in masonry supply yards) and set one atop the other with a mix of 1 part Portland cement to 3 parts sand, plus water. Use regular cement blocks, on their side, as the base for the grill; these are cemented together.

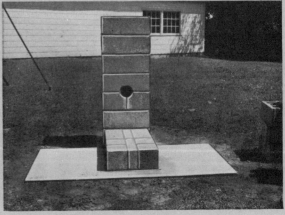

Photographs courtesy of Majestic Co., Inc.

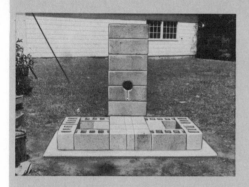

4. The wings for the barbecue are formed by setting a series of concrete blocks along the perimeter of the base. Use the 1:3 cement mix to hold blocks to base and to each other. Work carefully and make neat joints, using a pointed trowel or a short piece of pipe to produce a finished joint.

5. Since the grill unit will go in the center, build up both wings or sides by adding staggered rows of blocks upon each lower row. If your grill is 19″ wide, use a 3″ wide concrete block as a filler in the grill section. If the grill is only 15″ wide, this 3″ filler block can be omitted.

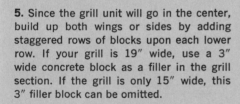

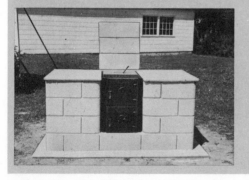

6. After three rows have been added above the base row for the wings, set a pre-formed concrete slab on top of each wing as a counter top. Secure with a 1:3 cement mix. The metal grill unit can be slipped into place between the two wings with the top level with the concrete slabs.

Attractive Barbecues For the Advanced Handyman

See how-to plans in this section; also see BRICK and CONCRETE.

One-Hour Barbecues

Rustic barbecues are easy and quick to make. These two models are particularly appropriate if you have just moved into your home and want a barbecue but don't have the time to build an elaborate one. Maybe, once you make either of these, you'll like it so much that you'll forget about that dream model.

Either of these two one-hour barbecues is made with brick. You need not use new brick. If you have some old brick about or can buy it cheaply in your area, you'll find that the old brick will add a certain decorative charm to that rustic appearance.

The pit for these units is dug out of the ground itself. Dig a hole about 8″ to 12″ deep. The circular model should be about 36″ in diameter and the rectangular rustic barbecue should be about 36″ long and about 20″ wide. In both, the outside border or perimeter is made of brick set in the ground so that one half of the brick extends above the earth's surface.

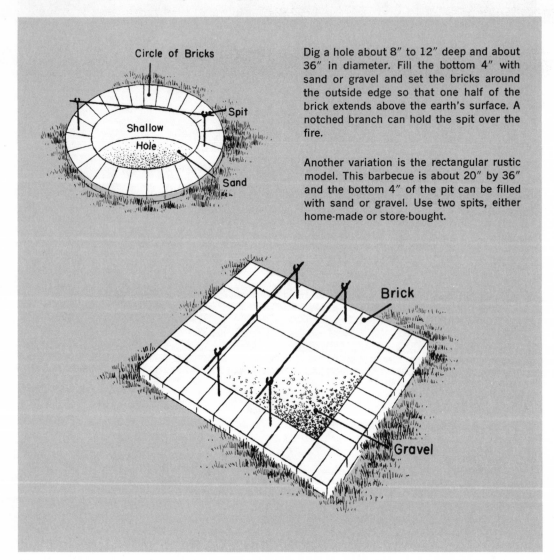

Circle of Bricks

Spit

Shallow Hole

Sand

Dig a hole about 8″ to 12″ deep and about 36″ in diameter. Fill the bottom 4″ with sand or gravel and set the bricks around the outside edge so that one half of the brick extends above the earth's surface. A notched branch can hold the spit over the fire.

Another variation is the rectangular rustic model. This barbecue is about 20″ by 36″ and the bottom 4″ of the pit can be filled with sand or gravel. Use two spits, either home-made or store-bought.

Brick

Gravel

Circular Barbecue

You can have lots of fun with your family and friends sitting around a circular barbecue. Here's a very easy one to make. All you need is an old 55 gallon oil drum and some cistern blocks.

Cut the oil drum to one fourth of its original height. The shallow section serves as the fire base for the unit. You can set it flush on the ground. The outside walls are made of a double row of cistern blocks, set with or without mortar, on the ground level flush against the outside of the oil drum.

¼ of Oil Drum

Cistern Blocks

This inexpensive circular barbecue can be built by the handyman in just about an hour. If you cannot get an old 55 gallon oil drum, any large metal can, over 20″ in diameter, will do. If you have small children about, use cement to hold the cistern blocks in place.

Grill-Warmer-Storage Unit

A few old bricks, some cement (either ready mixed or a 1:3 mix of Portland cement and sand) plus two iron grates are all you need to make this attractive barbecue. The center section is for the cooking of food. One side wing is for keeping the food warm over a small fire, while the other wing can be used for storage of wood.

This barbecue can be built directly on the ground. But if you live in an area of severe winters where the ground is apt to heave, dig down about 8″ and fill to within 1″ of the ground level with gravel and sand. Then build the unit on the top of this.

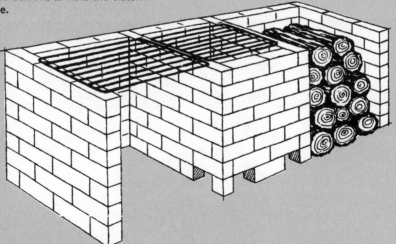

This combination barbecue can be built by the handyman in just a few hours. Leave two bricks out of the bottom row of the center unit to create the necessary draft for the fire. The iron grates are merely laid atop of the brick.

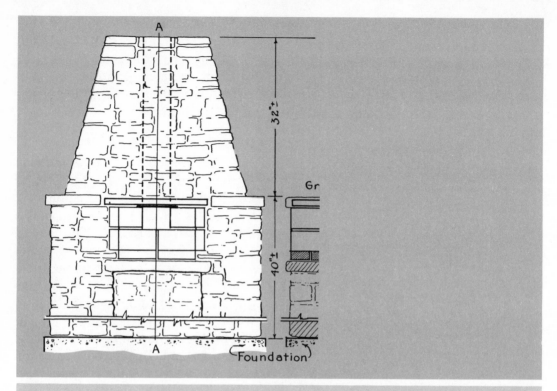

An attractive fireplace with a chimney for the advanced handyman. This barbecue certainly will be an eye-catcher in anyone's backyard. A foundation below the frost line is necessary to support a fireplace of this type.

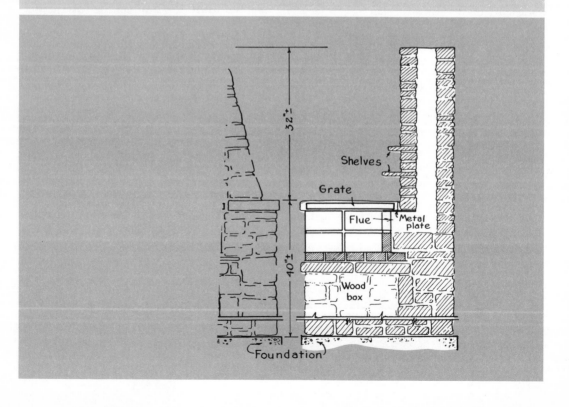

Bars

Have fun with a snack bar out-of-doors in the hot summer weather. This bar, without the casters on the underside, can also be used down in the basement recreation room in the winter.

A portable or built-in bar adds to the hospitality of the home when serving soft drinks for the teenagers or stronger beverages for the adult guests. The most appropriate place for the bar is in a recreation room, but it may also fit into the living or dining room, an alcove or foyer.

Converted Bars

A narrow table could easily be converted into a bar, by enclosing the front and two sides with plywood or wood boards, and leaving the back open. Build two shelves under the bar, of boards strong enough to carry the weight of glasses, bottles, and other necessary mixing apparatus. Paint or varnish the front and sides of the bar, and put a special liquid-proof finish on the top. Or you could cement to the surface a piece of left-over floor linoleum or a heavy plastic tabletop covering.

Enclosed bookshelves, which have a back and two sides, may also be converted into a bar. Turn the back of the bookshelves to face into the room, and use the shelves for all the glassware and mixings. Make the top, which is now the serving counter, liquid-proof through lacquering, varnishing or covering with a suitable material.

If you do not have much space to accommodate a bar, it could be placed on casters (one at each of its four corners) and rolled out when company arrives, then rolled away into an out-of-the-way spot when not in use.

Constructing a Bar

The length of the bar depends on the area you have available. A corner of the room is usually the best place to install the bar. The counter should be about 44″ from the floor; this is a convenient height to "bend the merry elbow" if the guests stand at the bar, and it is also good when they sit on the stools which are set in front of the bar.

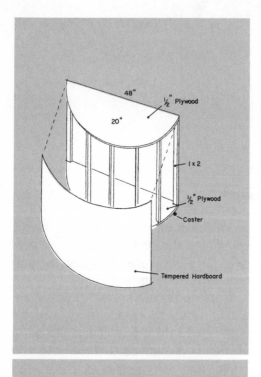

Details of the circular bar—top and bottom are cut out of ½″ plywood and vertical supports out of 1x2's. Secure plywood to supports with glue and two flathead screws, 1½″ long at each support. Countersink the screw heads. The ornamental face is glued and nailed to the plywood edges and the vertical supports. Casters are added to make the unit movable.

The counter width should be about 20 inches; if possible extend it an inch in front of the bar, and two inches over the back.

In building a bar, you could use up some second-hand lumber, or buy new wood or plywood. First build a framework of 2x4's of the height, width, and depth needed for the bar. Then cut the plywood or wood boards to fit the front and sides of the bar, and nail these to the framework. Cut two shelves to fit under the bar, and nail them in. Last, the counter top is cut, and fastened down over the completed bar. For the shelves and top use a hard wood to accommodate weight.

Finish the outside of the bar with paint or varnish; the counter top to be lacquered, varnished or plastic laminated.

Making a Curved Bar

Add zest to the season's out-of-door parties by serving from a portable snack bar. You can make this unit to fit inside your home as well. Everything can be served from a snack bar with a two-tone curved front covered with a decorative material such as Masonite Leatherwood.

The bar should be 44″ high, 48″ across the back and have a 20″ radius. The top and bottom are cut out of ½″ plywood to shape shown in sketch with 1x2's cut for vertical supports. Space these about 6″ to 9″ apart along the circumference of the curved edge. Cut the Leatherwood panel to size and glue and nail in place. Add 3 casters to the bottom for easy moving. For a two-tone finish, see section on *PAINTING*.

Plans for a Basic Bar with Many Surface Materials.

Maybe you'd like to stick to the traditional rectangular-shaped bar. Here is a simple, easy-to-make frame, which can be finished in a variety of ways to suit many tastes. Just follow the step-by-step plans noted in the accompanying illustrations.

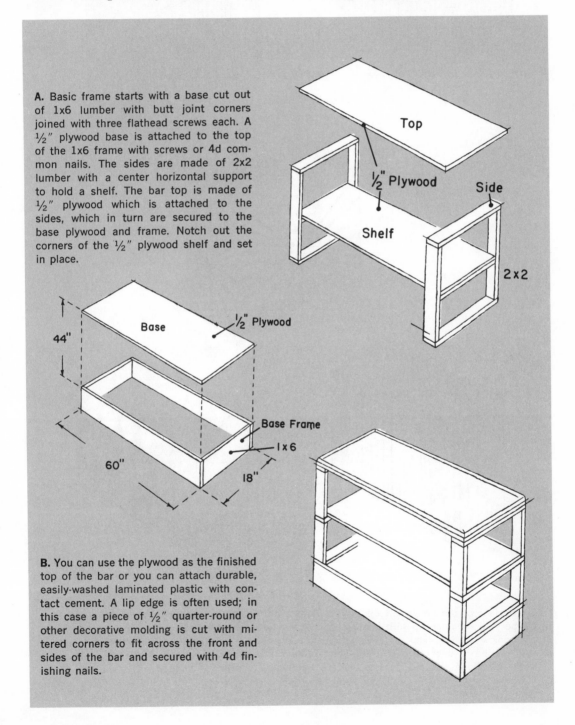

A. Basic frame starts with a base cut out of 1x6 lumber with butt joint corners joined with three flathead screws each. A ½" plywood base is attached to the top of the 1x6 frame with screws or 4d common nails. The sides are made of 2x2 lumber with a center horizontal support to hold a shelf. The bar top is made of ½" plywood which is attached to the sides, which in turn are secured to the base plywood and frame. Notch out the corners of the ½" plywood shelf and set in place.

Top

½" Plywood

Side

Shelf

2x2

Base

½" Plywood

44"

60"

18"

Base Frame

1x6

B. You can use the plywood as the finished top of the bar or you can attach durable, easily-washed laminated plastic with contact cement. A lip edge is often used; in this case a piece of ½" quarter-round or other decorative molding is cut with mitered corners to fit across the front and sides of the bar and secured with 4d finishing nails.

C. The face of the bar is left up to you. Here are 5 examples of what any handyman can do. Maybe you will come up with another type of your own choice. Those shown here are striated plywood, 1″ half-rounds, random-width tongue-and-groove pine or other type of lumber, tempered hardboard decorated in a sun-burst pattern of wood trim painted in a contrasting color to the hardboard, or floor tiles glued to a hardboard or plywood face added to the bar. Once the basic frame is built, you can apply any type of material to fit into your decorating scheme.

Base Molding

This molding is nailed along the top of a baseboard to give it a more attractive appearance.

Also see *BASEBOARD*.

Baseboard

The term baseboard is commonly used to describe the three component parts of the base trim which covers the seam between the wall and floor. Technically, however, it refers only to the main strip of wood without the base and shoe moldings. It must always be nailed through the wall to the studs.

If the top of the baseboard is not milled to give a finished appearance, a base molding may be added for decoration. It is nailed directly to the baseboard to prevent any separation between the two parts.

The last part to be added is the shoe molding which covers any gaps in the flooring as well as being decorative. It may be nailed either to the floor or the sub-flooring, if the latter extends far enough. It must never be attached to the baseboard directly since any shrinkage in the baseboard would cause the shoe molding to lift off the floor.

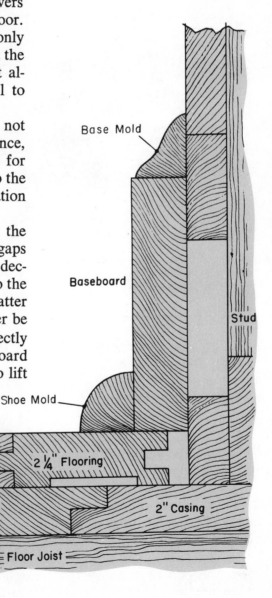

Base Mold

Baseboard

Stud

Shoe Mold

Finish Floor

2 1/4" Flooring

Subfloor

2" Casing

Floor Joist

Basements

The design and planning of this basement provides space for husband and wife to be near each other though busy with their own projects. In a basement area such as this the whole family can work and play together.

Photo courtesy makers of Armstrong's Asphalt Tile

Basements are the favorite location for rooms, for games, hobbies, entertainment and laundry facilities. The term game room has been closely identified with the basement conversions and today this term includes practically all the informal entertaining done by the family.

The first step in remodeling your basement will be to wall off sections for heating and laundry purposes. Your wall and ceiling facings will probably consist of composition boards, tiles, plywood or simulated woods and veneers.

If you are fortunate enough to have plastered brick walls you can finish with whitewash or any one of the special masonry paints. However, if yours is the average basement, you will need more work to make the basement suitable for all-purpose use. In addition, you will have to conceal plumbing, heating and wiring.

False walls and partitions are easily built of 2x4 wood studs to give you any of the dimensions you plan. They can also be used to cover any ugly objects as well as permitting the construction of shelving and built-ins.

Check the basement carefully for dampness and leaks. Before you begin your conversion project, it will be necessary to repair all cracks and leaks and use the special paints and mixtures to eliminate dampness.

In your selection of wallboards or wood facings choose facings with insulating and moisture resistant qualities.

A cement floor in good condition can be marked off in a flagstone or terrace effect. Various designs and patterns can be applied with the new basement floor paints available. When many of these new finishes are waxed they will give your basement floor a rich tiled effect. On concrete in contact with the earth, as asphalt tile floor covering is recommended.

First rate planning produced this child's playroom which is also a work and study area. Spacious under-bed storage drawers provide a bonus, while windows let in lots of fresh air and daylight. Dividers provide privacy as well.

Under other conditions, if no dampness is present, you may use flooring materials such as wood, cork, linoleum or various tiles.

Basement windows are always small and may be darkened by being set below the surface of the earth with small excavations for light. The daylight penetration for the basement can be increased by making larger excavations and using curtain material which does not cut off any of the light. The new translucent glass blocks as partitions between any of the room divisions will also permit the transmitting of all existing light.

You will probably have to extend the wiring to provide a sufficient quantity of light as well as outlets for the various activities planned for the room. Check your local building codes to determine whether or not you will need to have this work done by a licensed electrician. The electrical installations should be put in

Photo courtesy Armstrong Cork Co.

after you have erected the 2x4 studs but before the wall surfacing and ceiling material have been installed.

While you are planning the resurfacing of walls and ceiling be sure to allow for storage space and cabinets for all of the equipment, tools and games. Cabinets and closets for folding chairs, tables, games and the children's toys should be provided with plenty of shelves and hooks. Extra closets for outdoor and sports equipment should also be considered. Design your storage area with special racks and compartments to keep your gear in order.

A must in any basement game room is a bar, whether you serve liquor or soft drinks. You can provide a soft drink and milk bar for the younger set at the opposite end of the room or save a special section of your bar for them.

Another feature to consider is the possibility of basement cooking for indoor picnics. It may be possible to open a chimney and install a fireplace or you may want to build a cooking area around one of the new broiler-rotisseries. If there's an extra refrigerator or you can afford another one you may want to plan on a good location for it.

In a big airy basement you can combine all of the family hobbies and assign special sections to each member of the family and build special cabinets and work areas for the particular hobbies.

Decorating possibilities for the basement are unlimited; it is perhaps the one area in the house where you can try anything in color and design. Remember that this is an area for entertainment and activity and be guided by that.

Perhaps one of the best ways to plan a basement game and recreation room is to choose an interesting theme and build around it. You can gather an assortment of props which are appropriate to the theme and dramatize them in a decorative and interesting manner. You may want to plan on a nautical theme, a tavern, a western motif, use theatrical props or use your hobby as the basis for the decorating theme.

In planning your basement conversion there are an unlimited number of booklets, pamphlets and decorating suggestions available to you through your paint, hardware, lumber and building supply dealers.

Sealing the Walls

As mentioned earlier in this section one of the most common problems is dampness in the basement. Whether your basement is finished or unfinished and particularly before you launch your conversion project, here are some tips on how to keep your basement dry.

1. Seal the walls and floor with a cement paint which actually becomes part of the original masonry.

2. Leaking joints between basement walls and floor slab should be sealed with a mixture of cement paint and sand.

3. Relieve water pressure against outside of basement wall by sloping grade away from the house. Plant a dense turf to help shed the rain water and add tile extensions to the drain spouts.

4. Asphalt waterproofing compound and cement will solve many of the minor leakage problems in the basement.

5. If the floor shows damp spots,

The two photos show how clever planning in a basement can combine work and play areas. Laundries, usually located in the basement, can be incorporated in your planning without interfering with attractive decorating.

Photograph courtesy makers of Armstrong's Asphalt Tile

use a thick coating of asphalt, covered with 2″ of waterproof cement mortar.

6. Test for condensation by placing a small mirror against the wall. If droplets or fog appear on the mirror a few hours later, it means that condensation is the cause of some of your dampness.

7. Ventilation or air movement, by fans, will help to solve the condensation problem.

Also see *DAMPPROOFING A BASEMENT*.

Planning and Constructing a Basement Playroom

Below grade basement floors can be made warm and attractive by using the latest types of carpet designed for such purposes. Some kinds can be used outdoors as well. They come in many lovely patterns and colors.

Photo courtesy Armstrong Cork Company

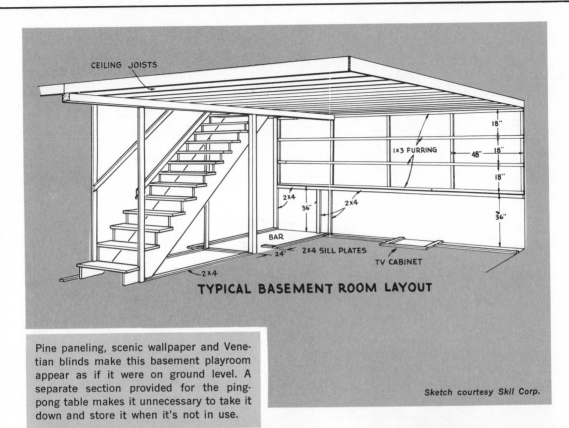

CEILING JOISTS

1x3 FURRING

18"

48" 18"

18"

36"

36"

2x4

2x4

BAR

24"   2x4 SILL PLATES

TV CABINET

2x4

TYPICAL BASEMENT ROOM LAYOUT

Pine paneling, scenic wallpaper and Venetian blinds make this basement playroom appear as if it were on ground level. A separate section provided for the ping-pong table makes it unnecessary to take it down and store it when it's not in use.

Sketch courtesy Skil Corp.

Photograph courtesy makers of Armstrong's Asphalt Tile

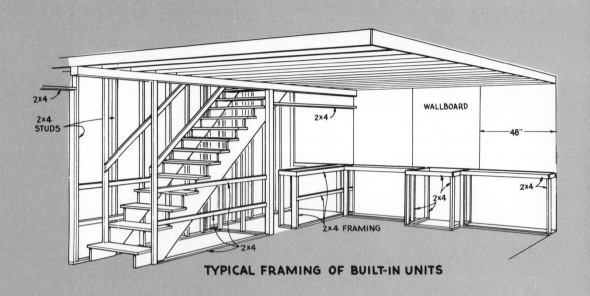

2x4

2x4
STUDS

2x4

WALLBOARD

48"

2x4

2x4

2x4 FRAMING

2x4

TYPICAL FRAMING OF BUILT-IN UNITS

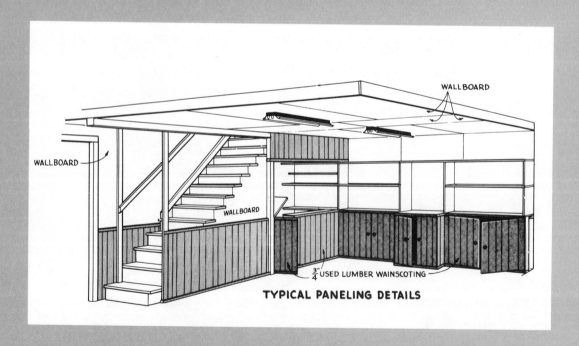

WALLBOARD

WALLBOARD

WALLBOARD

WALLBOARD

$\frac{3}{4}$" USED LUMBER WAINSCOTING

TYPICAL PANELING DETAILS

Sketches courtesy Skil Corp.

1. Plan the exact size of your room. Use a pencil and paper to work out you floor plan. A good scale is to have 1½″ equal 1′. Decide where the heating and laundry rooms will go if they are to be separted. Locate all of the partitions on your floor plan and keep in mind your plumbing and wiring arrangements in assigning space to the various activities.

2. Take your floor plans and any rough sketches with you to your lumber dealer. He will assist you with suggestions and latest information on construction materials. Although 2x4's are recommended, you can save some money by using 2x3's.

3. Nail the 2x4 sole plates to the floor at the wall and ceiling joints and wherever there are to be any partitions. Use steel cut 10-penny nails and a good heavy hammer.

4. Nail a 2x4 top plate under the ceiling joists.

5. The studs, all 2x4's, are nailed in place between the sole and top plates. Check very carefully with carpenter's level to make sure studs are vertical. In addition to nailing studs around the walls, studs must be nailed to top and sole plates where the partitions, if any, will jut out into the room.

6. Use of 2x4 studs will give you plenty of dead air space between cellar wall and wall surfacing material you will apply.

7. Once again, before you apply any of the wall surfacing, make sure that you have treated the cellar walls against dampness and that all leaks and cracks have been repaired.

8. Placement of studs on 16″ centers will give you a great deal of firm support; however, if you are using 4x8 panels and want to save some time and money, you can space them 24″ on center.

9. Assuming that you have chosen some form of wallboard or other type of wall covering which is available in 4x8 sheets you are ready to begin surfacing the wall. If you decide to decorate with vertical planking, you will also have to cover the walls with furring strips to give you a nailing surface.

10. One-inch brads are used to attach the wall surfacing material to the studs and joists. Before you go too far with your wall surface material, check all corners and angles to make sure that you have provided yourself with a nailing surface. You may have to add additional studs to give a nailing surface.

11. On certain wall surface materials it won't be necessary to countersink the nail heads. Wall materials such as *Surfwood, Leatherwood* and other rough textured materials will hide the nail heads and save you a good deal of time which you would have to spend in counter-sinking and filling nail holes.

12. Use 4′ panels and plan your work so that you have a minimum of cutting and fitting to do.

13. Fuse boxes, meters and other projections can be boxed in and covered over with the wall surfacing material or a contrasting material. Be sure that you permit access to these fixtures.

14. Use your 2x4 studs and wall covering material to make the bar, corner seats, storage benches, recessed light fixtures and for built-in cabinets and closets.

15. Windows are taken care of by nailing studding around the window, cutting the panels to fit around the

This unfinished basement contained a large amount of unused space. In re-decorating it, function was given first consideration. Counters and storage units built in around laundry appliances made the room into an efficient work center. Panel lights in a drop ceiling provided the necessary illumination.

Photograph courtesy Wood Conversion Co.

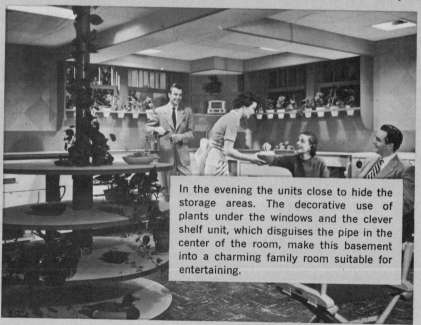

In the evening the units close to hide the storage areas. The decorative use of plants under the windows and the clever shelf unit, which disguises the pipe in the center of the room, make this basement into a charming family room suitable for entertaining.

frames and then trimming with picture frame molding; or cut strips from the wall surfacing material and trim with that.

Basement Playroom Ceiling

Although often omitted in basements, a ceiling improves the appearance, does away with numerous corners and spaces between joists where cobwebs and dust collect, and prevents dust from passing through the first-story flooring to the rooms above, especially where the floors are of a single thickness.

Of far greater importance, if the ceiling is of tight-fitting fire-resistant materials, is the safety it affords by delaying the spread of basement fire to floors above and by reducing smoke damage.

If the basement is dry and well built, it can often be made more attractive by installing a ceiling and painting the walls and floor. If the concrete floor is dry, it may be covered with asphalt tile to give a smooth, attractive floor which can be maintained with the minimum of effort by waxing.

Before putting on the ceiling, all openings through which fire might find quick passage to the structure above should be adequately fire-stopped. Such openings may be found around service pipes and registers and between joists or studs where they join the foundation. It is best to use incombustible materials for fire-stopping, such as crushed refuse mortar, plaster, concrete, hollow tile, gypsum block, broken brick, or other similar material that contains sufficiently fine particles to fill the voids. The firestopping can be supported by horizontal wood strips, not less than 2 inches thick, or by metal or wire mesh.

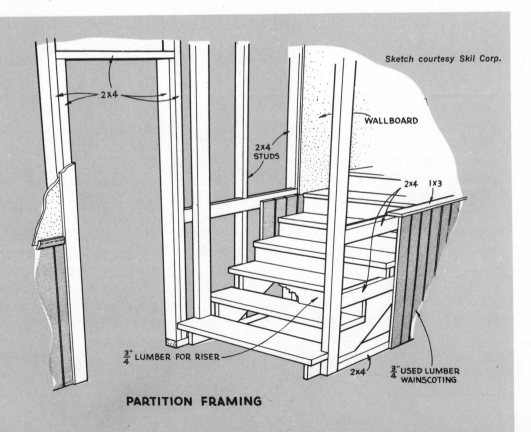

Sketch courtesy Skil Corp.

2X4

WALLBOARD

2X4 STUDS

2x4 1X3

¾" LUMBER FOR RISER

2x4   ¾" USED LUMBER WAINSCOTING

PARTITION FRAMING

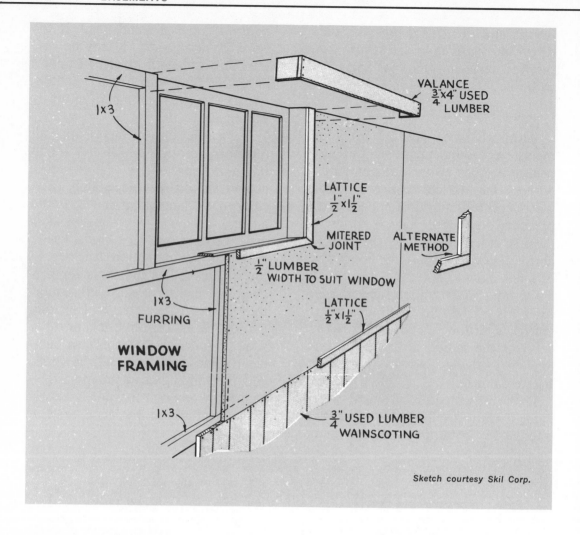

VALANCE
$\frac{3}{4}$"x4" USED
LUMBER

1x3

LATTICE
$\frac{1}{2}$"x1$\frac{1}{2}$"

MITERED
JOINT

ALTERNATE
METHOD

$\frac{1}{2}$" LUMBER
WIDTH TO SUIT WINDOW

1x3
FURRING

LATTICE
$\frac{1}{2}$"x1$\frac{1}{2}$"

**WINDOW
FRAMING**

1x3

$\frac{3}{4}$" USED LUMBER
WAINSCOTING

Sketch courtesy Skil Corp.

Several materials are used for ceiling purposes: Gypsum- or asbestosboard, hardboard, plywood or ceiling tiles of various materials may be used, depending upon the taste of the individual and the amount of money to be spent.

Material within 2′ of the top of a boiler or furnace, or within 1′ of a smoke pipe, should be protected by a loose-fitting metal shield, arranged to give an air space of 1″ or 2″ between the metal and the wall surface. The air space may be provided by using small blocks of incombustible material between metal and joists, or by suspending the metal sheets on wires or hooks fastened to the joists.

If tin is used for a shield, it should have locked joints, since soldered joints are not reliable. Similar protection should be placed over any woodwork or wood lath and plaster partition, within 4′ of the sides or back, or 6′ from the front, of any boiler, furnace, or other heating equipment. This covering should extend at least 4′ above the floor and at least 3′ beyond the heating device on all sides.

1. A variety of ceiling materials is available to you. If your ceiling

Before

Here is an extensive project which turned the basement into a master bedroom. Grading exposed the rear wall of the basement and sliding glass doors to the patio were installed. Window above bed was extended to let in more light and air.

Photograph courtesy makers of Armstrong's Temlock

After

joists are 16″ on center you can nail the 16″ x 16″ tiles directly to the joists without nailing up furring strips. If you want a diagonal design or a pattern you will have to nail up furring strips and work out your pattern on paper first.

2. Special clips are available for securing the tiles to the ceiling. You can also use box nails or staples.

3. If you are going to have a music room in the basement or work with power tools or even for entertaining, you would be wise to consider using a soundproofing ceiling material. It may cost you a few cents more, but the benefits to the family upstairs will be well worth the investment.

Also see *CEILING TILES.*

Basement Playroom Flooring

A variety of floor covering materials are available to finish off your basement project. You can use wood, tile, paint or other types of linoleum and inlay. Since there will probably be a great deal of activity in the basement playroom and the flooring will be subject to heavy traffic choose a sturdy long-lasting material. If you will check with your flooring dealer you will find that it is possible to get inlays to use on the floor, for shuffleboard and other games.

You will find that a good tile is recommended and preferred for the basement floor. Rubber and asphalt are the most popular though a vinyl plastic has been developed.

Also see *FLOOR TILES*.

Tips on Laying Tile Flooring

1. Snap a chalk line across the center of the floor. Various patterns and designs are suggested by the manufacturer and instructions are packaged with the tiles.

2. Use a toothed trowel to spread the adhesive. Floor must show between grooves for a perfect bonding.

3. After the adhesive has dried according to the manufacturers instructions snap your chalk guide lines over again.

4. Your first tile is placed at the spot where the lines cross in the center of the room.

This tavern style recreation room is made doubly attractive by the use of the new "Flagstone" asphalt tile. These new tiles are laid by using a "grid-unit" to place them accurately.

Photograph courtesy Armstrong Cork Co.

Before

A roomy basement is shown on right; its bareness makes it unattractive. The transformation makes it a cheerful, pleasant place in which to work and entertain. The long bench at the rear is simply poured concrete behind a brick facing.

Photograph courtesy makers of Armstrong's Asphalt Tile

After

5. Fill a quarter of the area at a time, each time returning to the center to start over again.

6. Leave the area butting against the wall until last. Unless the tiles fit perfectly from one wall to the other you will have to trim the tiles individually for a good fit.

7. Tiles are cut by scoring with a linoleum knife and then breaking the tile by snapping across a sharp edge.

8. Blowtorch, hot radiator, or furnace will heat asphalt tiles before laying and make cutting easier. Stack the tiles flat when heating them. Keep

them clean and free of adhesive.

9. Dividers are used to mark tiles to cut borders and to fit around obstructions and pipes.

10. Follow manufacturer's recommendations for waxing and preserving tiles.

Hints and Suggestions for Basement Planning and Construction

A check list of the activities you plan to carry on in the basement will save you a great deal of time and effort in planning the conversion. Although there are a great number of activities which can be undertaken in the basement the following general list should help you plan your project.

On the basis of the ideas and activities listed you should now be able to prepare a plan which will provide space and storage facilities for the equipment necessary for the activities checked.

CHECKLIST
- . . . . Music Room
- . . . . Record collection
- . . . . Workshop
- . . . . Laundry & Ironing
- . . . . Soda Counter
- . . . . Games Area
- . . . . Handicrafts & Hobbies
- . . . . Garment Storage
- . . . . Extra Bedroom
- . . . . Snack Bar
- . . . . Darkroom
- . . . . Gardening Corner
- . . . . Still and Motion Picture Projection
- . . . . Reading Area, Library
- . . . . Arts & Crafts Section
- . . . . Teener's Club Room
- . . . . Sewing Center
- . . . . TV Area
- . . . . Stamp Collection
- . . . . Display Areas

Before

A drab, crowded basement, treated with a nautical theme, becomes a colorful and spacious recreation area for youngsters and adults. A small alcove with a built-in work bench and overhead light becomes a cozy corner for dad and junior to work on projects together.

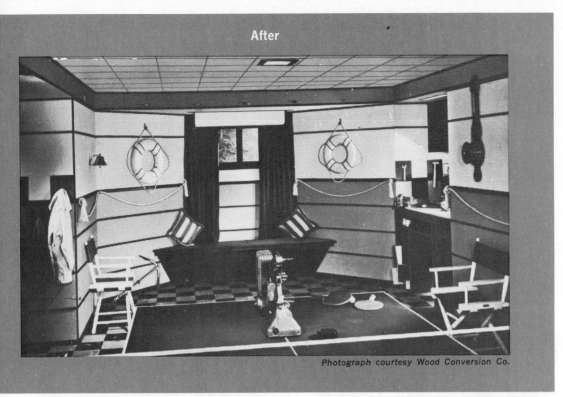

After

Photograph courtesy Wood Conversion Co.

The following suggestions will help you to organize your basement conversion project:

1. Plan a functional basement playroom. Materials and decorating scheme will depend upon what you plan to do there.

2. Plan areas like the darkroom or kitchen or gardening corner near the plumbing to save on the amount of pipe you will need.

3. If you plan a sewing center remember to provide a cutting table.

4. Built-ins are inexpensive, functional, and easy to tailor to your specific needs. You can plan and design work surfaces, walls and other furnishings which will do double duty.

5. Hidden light sources and reflected lights will dramatize your decorations. Make use of recessed lights and spots as well as the fluorescent tubes.

6. Shift the furnace into a corner of the basement. If this cannot be done, enclose it, using decorative asbestos to cover it over.

7. Study various plans and designs for your stairway. Make it a part of your basement decoration rather than just a means to go up and down.

8. Bring the outdoors inside. Use planters and plenty of greenery to add life to the room. Various types of

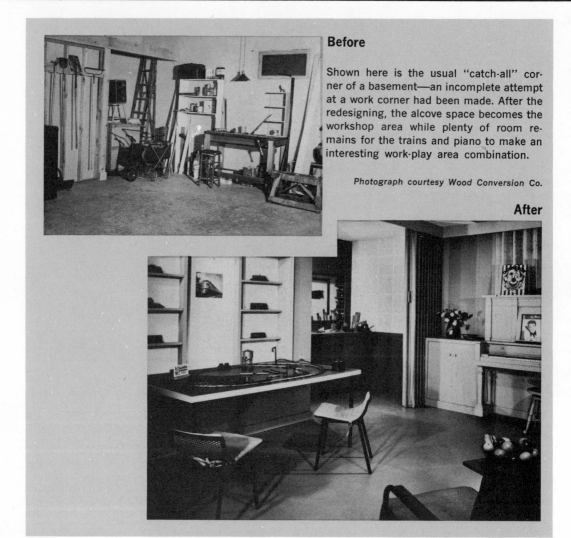

Before

Shown here is the usual "catch-all" corner of a basement—an incomplete attempt at a work corner had been made. After the redesigning, the alcove space becomes the workshop area while plenty of room remains for the trains and piano to make an interesting work-play area combination.

Photograph courtesy Wood Conversion Co.

After

building blocks and other brick and concrete can be used to make partial room dividers for plants and flowers.

9. Make use of a variety of bamboo, dowels, slats and folding doors to create screens and sliding doors to save space.

10. While you are setting up the sole plates for the partitions make the necessary provisions for the type of doors you intend to use.

11. Use a carpenter's level to check studs, furring strips and all other vertical and horizontal wood members you are installing.

12. Glass blocks can be utilized as partitions. They can be set up with wood strips or mortar. Check the manufacturer's recommendations for installation. Glass block partitions will permit the passage of light and still give privacy.

13. Many of the new wall materials designed for use in the basement as well as in other rooms in the house require no finishing. They will save you time and money if you utilize them.

Here's a list of some of the types available:

SHEETS
  Fiberboard
  Plasterboard
  Insulating wallboard
  Hardboard
  Asbestos wallboard
  Perforated hardboard
  Plywood

BLOCKS AND BRICKS
  Glass
  Plastic
  Red bricks
  Cinder blocks
  Fieldstone

PANELS
  Insulating panels
  Corrugated Fiberglas
  Wood planks
  Perforated steel
  Rigid plastic board
  Glass

Sound absorbing acoustical tile was used on the ceiling of this basement playroom. The tile's surface is smooth and easy to keep clean. Jam sessions in this playroom won't keep the whole neighborhood awake.

Photograph courtesy makers of Armstrong's Asphalt Tile

14. Special clips and other types of fasteners have been designed to speed up the job of installing wall surfacing material. Some of the different types are listed.

15. The door and window trim are added after the wall surfacing material has been attached.

Also see *DOOR FRAMING*.

16. When working with panels, put up a corner panel but cut the edges to fit any of the wall irregularities. Then the outer edge of this panel becomes the guide for the following panels.

17. Cove moldings at the ceiling-wall and floor-wall joints will cover up any mistakes and unsightly joints. 8-penny finishing nails are used to put up moldings, nail heads are countersunk and the holes filled and sanded before painting or staining.

18. Do as much painting as possible on walls and ceilings before the moldings are put up to prevent splashes and spots.

19. With your heating pipes and ducts, it will be simpler and less expensive for you if you leave them where they are and box them in.

20. Be sure to allow space for complete insulation before enclosing any steam pipe.

WALL	FASTENER
Hardboard	¾″ flat-headed sheet metal screws
Tongue-and-groove board	2″ flooring nails
Rigid plastic panels	1″ finishing nails or molding strips
Asbestos wallboard	5-penny coated nails
Plywood	1¼″ finishing nails
Fiberboard	1¼″ steel nails

The basement project is a task which can be completed in two or three week-ends or it can take as much time as you are willing to give to it. Remember to measure and check your measurements before you cut any of your material. If you have any questions or problems take sketches and measurements to your lumber yard or building supply dealer and he will help you.

Also see *BUILT-INS, CEILING TILES, FLOORS, WALLS, ELEC-TRICAL WIRING*.

Basin Wrench

Used in plumbing, the wrench is necessary when fixtures are in difficult-to-reach places. The basin wrench is very much like an offset screwdriver—it does the job where the standard tool cannot be used. In most homes a basin wrench is needed only when connecting or disconnecting faucets from a sink or when working on bathtub faucets that are built into the wall.

The basin wrench has a reversible action lever. The toothed, curved section that grips the plumbing fixture can be removed and reinserted in the stem to work in either a clockwise or counter-clockwise direction. The top handle slides through a slot in the major stem so that extra pres-

sure can be exerted when necessary. In extreme cases it is permissible to use a short length of pipe over this handle for added leverage to "break" a tight joint.

Also see *WRENCHES*.

Bass Reflex

This type of speaker enclosure is the simplest for the handyman to build. It consists of two sides, a top and bottom and a front and back panel, plus a circular opening for the speaker and a rectangular port opening below the circular opening.

The size of a bass reflex cabinet varies depending upon the size and type of speaker you use. You can get full information about the cubic content needed for your speaker from the manufacturer. He will also supply you with the dimensional data for the circular and rectangular openings.

A bass reflex cabinet extends the bass characteristic of the speaker to a new low and broadens the speaker resonance to a moderate degree, re-

sulting in a smoother over-all response.

When making your own cabinet, use ¾″ plywood or 1″ stock for thin or flimsy wood will vibrate and you will not get the full sound value out of the enclosure. Furthermore, join the top, sides and front with adhesive and screws. The back panel can be screwed into position so that it is easy to remove should you need to get at the speaker.

Some hi-fi fans prefer to line the inside of the enclosure with an insulating material. Normally, this is not needed unless you have an extremely powerful speaker that causes the parts to vibrate.

1. When making a bass reflex cabinet, select the size best suited for your individual speaker. The enclosure should be somewhat between 6 and 10 cubic feet. Here are a few guide measurements for proper proportions:

- A—width of the unit should be at least one half as large as B.
- B—height of the unit is generally about 25″ to 30″,
- C—the depth of the unit should be at least 12″ but 16″-18″ is preferred.
- D—the circular opening is determined by the size of the speaker. It is usually about 1″ smaller than the diameter of the speaker.
- E—the port or rectangular opening is placed directly below the speaker hole. Its exact size is governed by the speaker; this data will be supplied by the speaker manufacturer.

2. When building a bass reflex, use ¾″ plywood or 1″ stock. Cut all the parts to size required, noting the assembly detail in the diagram. The top and bottom pieces fit in between the sides. The front panel is attached to fit over the sides, top and bottom. Note that the rear edge of the top and bottom are rabbet cut and the back fits into this space. The parts, aside from the back, should be secured with 1½″ #9 flathead screws plus adhesive. The back panel should be attached in the rabbet with 1½″ #6 screws spaced about 3″ to 4″ apart. Drill a hole in the back panel to permit speaker wire to pass through. This opening should be as small as possible. Cover the speaker and port openings with radio grille cloth by stapling the material to the inside of the front piece.

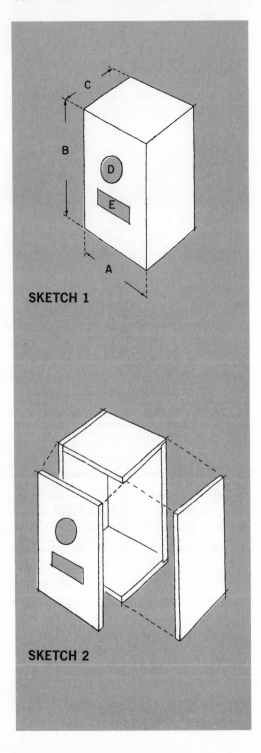

SKETCH 1

SKETCH 2